DEE BROWN, who is presently Librarian at the University of Illinois at Urbana, has won national fame for his *Bury My Heart at Wounded Knee*, perhaps the best selling book ever written about the American Indian, and has written many other works dealing with the West and its development.

MARTIN F. SCHMITT is a picture researcher whose patience and scholarship turned up the many hitherto-unknown photographs and other pictures for this and other books. He has also collaborated with Dee Brown on *Trail Driving Days and Settlers' West*.

Also by Dee Brown and Martin F. Schmitt on the
Ballantine Books List:

TRAIL DRIVING DAYS

THE SETTLERS' WEST

available at your local bookstore

FIGHTING INDIANS OF THE WEST

DEE BROWN
AND
MARTIN F. SCHMITT

BALLANTINE BOOKS · NEW YORK

FOR MARTHA AND SARA

Illustrated format:
First Printing: May, 1974

Regular edition:
First Printing: July, 1975

Cover art by Eva Cellini

Printed in the United States of America

BALLANTINE BOOKS
A Division of Random House, Inc.
201 East 50th Street, New York, N.Y. 10022
Simultaneously published by
Ballantine Books, Ltd., Toronto, Canada

PREFACE

CHIEF CREDIT FOR this book must go to the small group of intrepid photographers of the West who recorded with the magic of light and chemistry the actors and scenes and sometimes even the actions in the great historical drama of the Indian Wars.

As contributors of basic documents to American history, photographers have suffered a strange fate. Their records are second only to reality, yet historians have passed them by for millions of words—good, bad, and indifferent. Students of western history can name a hundred diary keepers and writers of official reports, but few of them seem to know the names of A. Z. Schindler, C. W. Carter, L. A. Huffman, DeLancey Gill, W. S. Soule, Camillus S. Fly, T. H. O'Sullivan, Ben Wittick, A. F. Randall, David F. Barry, G. E. Trager, Frank Currier, S. J. Morrow, D. D. Dare, O. S. Goff, John C. H. Grabill, Jack Hillers, Christian Barthelmess, or Louis Heller.

These and other photographers produced the stuff of history, and to the best of our ability we have attempted to give them individual credit for their contributions to this pictorial narrative.

We wish also to express our sincere appreciation to another small group of pioneers—the librarians and archivists who have recognized the value of photographs as historical records. Many a photograph included in this book is here only because of some librarian's alertness, vigilance, and historical sense.

We owe a tremendous debt to friends who made suggestions and offered leads to other sources. We are particularly proud to acknowledge the help of Mrs. Hermine Baumhofer of the National Archives and Miss Mae Clark of the Smithsonian Institution. Miss

Miriam B. Ketchum of the Bureau of American Ethnology Library was also more than cooperative.

The directors and staffs of the National Archives, Bureau of American Ethnology, Library of Congress, Nebraska Historical Society, Kansas Historical Society, Wyoming Historical Society, Denver Public Library, Missouri Historical Society, South Dakota Historical Society, Museum of the University of South Dakota, State Historical Society of Colorado, Title Insurance and Trust Company of Los Angeles, and the Laboratory of Anthropology at Santa Fe all show an uncommon interest in and respect for photographs. Their assistance is gratefully acknowledged. The List of Illustrations incorporates a full statement of specific credits.

Dr. Elmo Scott Watson of Northwestern University, one of the few authorities on western photographs, offered valuable suggestions. And without the basic study of American photography made by Dr. Robert Taft of Kansas, much of this work would not have been done.

DEE BROWN
MARTIN F. SCHMITT

CONTENTS

War Chief's Lodge, Shoshone Camp in Wind River Mountains. Along the streams of the West, the Indians pitched their tipis and lived as free as men have ever lived, bound only by the earth and the sky. Roaming herds of bison and elk were sacred animals, providing food, shelter, and clothing. The hunting grounds were sacred earth. And in the words of an old song:

> *"In a sacred manner I live*
> *To the heavens I gazed*
> *In a sacred manner I live*
> *My horses are many."*

INTRODUCTION

WITH THE ENDING of the Civil War in 1865, one of the most colorful periods in American history began. These were the lusty and rugged years of national expansion, of the westward migration. In the countless legends of the '70's and '80's, the gold seekers, the frontiersmen, and the United States cavalrymen have usually been the heroes.

But the Indians also were heroic, and the story of their long but futile struggle to keep their bison and their elk, their earth and their sky, is an epic that needs no romancer's gloss.

The story of the advancing frontier and retreating Indian, told in hundreds of personal narratives and official reports, was also recorded by the pioneer photographers, who arrived soon after the dust of the first great emigrant trains settled along the Platte River.

Daguerreotype, succeeded by various wet plate processes, was the medium of the early artists in the West. The surviving negatives and prints bear testimony to the handicaps imposed by such slow methods. Pioneer photographers carried all their equipment on muleback or in wagons—portable photographic laboratories, including an astonishing variety of materials from glass plates to iodine. Each view involved unpacking, sensitizing a plate, exposing the plate, developing on the spot, and then repacking. When such labor was accompanied by threats of Indian attacks, sandstorms, and other hazards of frontier travel, it becomes the more surprising that pictorial records were obtained at all.

Unfortunately, much of the work of pioneer photographers has literally gone up in smoke, and the re-

Buffalo Grazing. *"This nation, this buffalo nation—"*
For as long as the tribal calendars had recorded the seasons, the hooves of the buffalo had been drumming against the western earth.

"The buffaloes I, the buffalos I,
 I make the buffaloes march around;
 I am related to the buffaloes, the buffaloes."

Not only was the buffalo a symbol of food, shelter, and clothing—he was a symbol of life after death. In the body of each buffalo dwelt a manitou.

2

mainder is scattered in collections all over the United States, or lies, often unrecognized, in the possession of individuals.

The pictorial story which follows is made up largely of the best of these photographs, with occasional use of contemporary paintings and drawings to complete sequences for which no photographs exist. To understand this story, to comprehend the reasons for the action which is portrayed, it is necessary to know something of what occurred before the story begins.

Between the gold rush days of 1849 and the beginning of the Civil War, thousands of emigrants had been crossing the plains each year, seeking gold, opening trading posts, settling new farms. The Indians of the northwest had generally accepted the government's loose policy that all the land west of the "big bend of the Missouri" was theirs, and they expected the settlers to keep out. But in order to reach the rich mines and lands of the Far West, the pioneers had to cross territory which the Plains tribes considered sacred hunting grounds. Conflicts resulted. There were fights, and men were killed.

To meet the demands of the western travelers, army posts were set up along the main routes—the Oregon Trail and the Santa Fe Trail.

As more settlers crossed the Mississippi River into the rich farming lands west of the Great Lakes, large tracts of territory belonging to the Indians were declared open for homesteading. And although the dispossessed Indians received annuities as "compensation" for their losses, the agreements were not always carried out. Border incidents occurred with increasing frequency.

The Indians were beginning to remember the past. For two centuries, tribe after tribe had been forced westward, as treaties had been made and broken by the government with complete disregard of the Indians' rights. But the leaders of the Great Plains tribes, the Sioux in particular, were great travelers. They had seen many things and had heard much talk,

After the Buffalo Run. But the white men were coming to kill them by the thousands, destroying the sacred buffaloes by the thousands . . .

Indian Runner.   The western Indians knew that eventually they must fight for their lands. They remembered the treaties made and then so easily broken. They remembered the promises spoken by men with crooked tongues. From runners they learned that gold-seekers and adventurers were driving new trails across their beloved hunting grounds.

and they no longer believed in the white man's promises.

They were brave men, the Sioux. They realized that there must be an end to retreats if their way of life was to survive. They did not like the railroad spurs that were beginning to jut across the Mississippi, pointing significantly westward toward the rolling prairies. They hated the settlements that were rising rapidly along the lengthening trails and stage lines. They knew that in the rich lands of Minnesota, a band of their own tribe had been forced into a narrow, defenseless reserve along the Minnesota River.

When the white men began their Civil War in 1861, the forts and cantonments of the West were drained of experienced soldiers. The untrained volunteers who took their places were not equal to the native warriors of the plains. In August, 1862, a band of irresponsible braves killed five settlers near New Ulm, Minnesota, and loosed a series of bloody encounters between Indians and pioneers. Finally the Minnesotans organized a militia, and after a small battle, four hundred of the captive Indians were brought into St. Paul. They were tried, and most of them were sentenced to death. When Little Crow, a Sioux chieftain, tried to fight back, he was killed. His tanned scalp, his skull and his wristbones were put on exhibition.

Now the bars were down.

Twenty-five years of bloody conflict had been started, and the Sioux would be fighting to the end, until the day of final tragedy at Wounded Knee, South Dakota, December 29, 1890.

During the last months of the Civil War, conditions became so desperate for the settlers that in some sections west of the Mississippi, the Federal army was forced to use paroled Confederate prisoners to man the forts. By 1864, the Arapahoes and the Cheyennes had joined the Sioux and were raiding the trails along the South Platte and making forays into Nebraska. In November of that year, nine hundred Colorado militiamen made a surprise raid on the Arapaho and

The Chiefs Approach.   The Leaders said: The free open prairies and the sky-high mountains must not be traded for the worthless offerings of the white men. The tribal rites and customs, the sacred dances and the ceremonies must not be swallowed up in the ways of the white men. Let us follow the trail of our fathers. Let us guard the hunting grounds of our people.

Hoka Hey!   The Medicine Men chanted: "The earth is weeping, weeping." The old men of the tribes held councils and made many smokes and talked.

But the young warriors were angry. They smeared their bodies and the skins of their swift ponies with sacred medicine paint. They donned their war-bonnets and their gaudy war-shirts and all the emblems of battle peculiar to each tribe. They chanted war songs and danced war dances.

In little bands, without organization, they began to attack the invaders of their hunting grounds. But disciplined and well-armed soldiers of the government brushed them aside, and the pioneers and gold-seekers kept moving westward.

7

Little Crow. In August 1862 in Minnesota, a series of massacres took the lives of more than seven hundred settlers in a week. The Minnesotan militia captured two thousand Indians. Chief Little Crow maintained a fighting retreat up the Minnesota River, but his warriors were routed by General Henry H. Sibley near the Missouri Coteau in 1863. Little Crow was killed.

Cheyenne camp at Sand Creek, killing over one hundred men, women, and children. The beaten Indians were presented with a new treaty, and pushed farther back.

The strong Sioux tribes in the Dakotas, Montana, and Wyoming had been left almost unmolested through all these events. But they had watched the encroaching white men with wary eyes, and they were determined to resist any invasion of their finest hunting grounds with all the force they could muster. Red Cloud was one of the leaders, and he was a fighting chief.

The time for action came late in 1865, when the government decided to open a road to the Montana goldfields along the Bozeman Trail from Cheyenne northwestward to the headwaters of the Missouri. In the summer of 1865, General P. E. Connor and Jim Bridger with several hundred soldiers were sent on a march, now known as the Powder River Indian Expedition, to prepare the way for the new road. The soldiers were continually harassed by superior forces under Red Cloud's leadership, and the expedition finally was abandoned, the army withdrawing when General Connor was suddenly removed from his command.

Early the following year, Colonel Henry B. Carrington was sent into the Powder River country with a regiment of regular infantry. His orders were to open the Bozeman road, either peaceably or forcibly. Carrington arranged a meeting with the Sioux at Fort Laramie, and after considerable delay Red Cloud agreed to attend. At the conference, the proud Sioux chieftain drew his blanket closely about him and disdained an introduction to the military leaders.

In the midst of the negotiations, Red Cloud rose suddenly and faced Colonel Carrington: "You are the White Eagle who has come to steal the road! The Great Father sends us presents and wants us to sell him the road, but the White Chief comes with soldiers to steal it before the Indian says yes or no! I will talk with you no more! I will go, now, and I will fight you! As long as I live, I will fight you for the last hunting grounds of my people!"

With these words, Red Cloud turned and walked out of the council. Not many days would pass before the white men would know the meaning of what he had spoken.

Colonel Henry B. Carrington, Eighteenth Infantry. In 1866, Carrington was assigned the task of building and organizing a system of forts along the Bozeman Trail in Wyoming. While he was not entirely convinced of the rightness of what the government was doing, he made efficient arrangements for supply and defense. He believed in transferring the amenities of civilization to the frontier—including a forty-piece brass band, a mowing machine for the drill field, and a dozen rocking chairs. Carrington's greatest weakness was his lack of knowledge about the Indians.

RED CLOUD
OF THE SIOUX

I

RED CLOUD'S SCOUTS kept him well informed as to the movements of Colonel Carrington and the Eighteenth Infantry, from the day the soldiers marched out of Fort Laramie until they reached the Powder River country.

The Sioux leader knew that Carrington's force consisted of about 700 men, a number of civilian woodcutters and choppers, a scanty supply of ammunition, a forty-piece brass band, a dozen rocking chairs, a small beef herd, pigs and chickens, and machinery and tools for building a fort. He knew that wily old Jim Bridger was the guide and trusted adviser of the colonel. Red Cloud also must have guessed that the officers had not been impressed by his threats. Five of them, including Colonel Carrington, brought their wives and children along as confidently as if they were going on a summer outing instead of trespassing into hostile hunting grounds.

But when the expedition arrived at Fort Connor (soon to be renamed Fort Reno), they received a warning of what was in store for them. Raiding Indians captured nearly all the horses and mules assigned to Fort Reno, and an attack was also made on a civilian wagon train farther up the trail.

A few days later, after marching through July heat

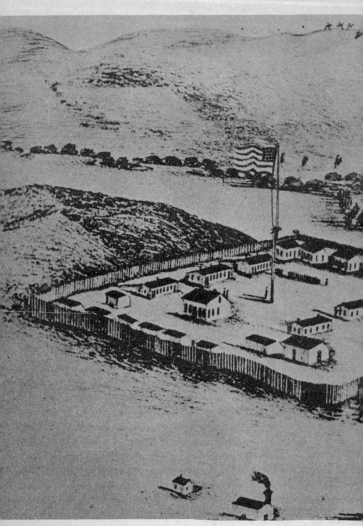

Fort Phil Kearny. In July, 1886, Carrington's men began building sturdy Fort Phil Kearny on the Little Piney Fork. But all through the summer and autumn, soldiers and civilian workers were slain intermittently by Red Cloud's lurking braves. Carrington's selection of the site revealed his ignorance of Indian fighting.

12

that caused the spokes of their wagon to break loose, the expedition finally reached Dry Creek. Here they made another contact with the sudden violence that stalked their advance. In the dry basin of the water hole at the camp site, they found the scalped and naked body of a dead white man.

Vigilance was redoubled. After they reached Crazy Woman's Fork, some of the men deserted and headed for the Montana goldfields. When a detail of soldiers was sent in pursuit, they were stopped by a band of Red Cloud's scouts and forbidden to proceed farther. In addition, a message from the Indians was sent back to Carrington, ordering him to take his soldiers out of the country. "It must be either peace or war," Red Cloud said. "If you want peace, return at once to Powder River."

But Carrington chose to march on to the Little Piney Fork, where he pitched his tents and started immediately to building Fort Phil Kearny. Although the army officers had brought with them complete plans for a model fort, the site they selected clearly demonstrated their lack of practical knowledge concerning Indian warfare. There was no cover between the fort and its water supply; the nearest fuel and timber supply was five miles distant; and high hills on all sides shut off observation of surrounding terrain. Jim Bridger wanted to march on to the Tongue River, but he was overruled by the military.

Meanwhile, two companies were dispatched northwards to construct a smaller fort, C. F. Smith. With Fort Reno behind him as a link to Laramie, Carrington had three forts along the Bozeman Trail. But his men were spread thin. He needed reinforcements, and Red Cloud knew that.

The strategy of the Sioux leader soon became clear. He made no mass attacks. He bided his time, sniping from the brush, picking off a man here, a man there, utilizing the old guerrilla tactics of the Indians. He hoped to cut the ranks of the well-armed invaders to a point where they would be forced either to withdraw

14

from the hunting grounds or to present so weak a front that the Sioux could destroy them in one final smashing attack.

Carrington, however, was a cautious strategist himself, even if he knew nothing about fighting Indians. He forbade his men to venture out in individual or small detachments. Every movement from the fort on the Little Piney was well guarded. Carrington also determined to build an impregnable fort, to perfect a defensive stronghold which no attacking force could storm. From the day the site was selected, the energies of every man, soldier and civilian alike, were devoted to the construction of the fort. The plans had been drawn up back in Nebraska, and the proper dimensions were staked out on the morning of July 15. Tents were pitched in rows where the buildings were to be constructed; a crude mowing machine which had been hauled all the way from Laramie clipped the grass for the parade ground; woodchoppers and armed soldiers moved out to begin cutting the logs for construction of the thick loopholed walls. By evening of that first day, Red Cloud's scouts on Lodge Trail Ridge, overlooking the fort, must have been amazed at what they saw below them.

The rapidity of the military invasion threatened to break apart Red Cloud's loosely integrated forces. The Blackfeet and the Crows had never accepted him as a leader, and the Cheyennes were vacillating in their allegiance.

Early on the morning of July 16, a few Cheyennes appeared on the hills above the long rectangle of army tents. When they displayed white flags, Colonel Carrington sent out a messenger to welcome them. Meanwhile, he ordered his men to prepare a grand reception in the largest hospital tents so as to dazzle the expected visitors.

As about forty Cheyenne chiefs, warriors, and squaws approached the encampment, the Eighteenth Infantry band marched out to greet them with a rousing military tune. The Cheyennes were impressed.

Black Horse and Dull Knife, wearing elaborate bears' claws necklaces and brilliant beaded moccasins, made long harangues. It was obvious that the Cheyenne chiefs were both fearful and jealous of the influence of the Sioux; they were trying to drive a bargain with the army. Red Cloud's followers, they informed Carrington, were at that moment having a sun-dance. And on the previous day, the Sioux had made a vain effort to induce the Cheyennes to make common cause with them in driving the white men back to Powder River.

The Cheyennes' inclination to make a strong peace with the white men was probably strengthened by the arrival of four additional companies of infantry late in the afternoon.

But only two days after the pow-wow with the Cheyennes, the Sioux made a raid on one of the Fort Kearny outposts, seizing several horses. When troops went in pursuit, they were ambushed. Before they could escape, two soldiers were killed, three wounded. About the same time that the casualties were brought in, bad news arrived from farther up the Bozeman Trail. A wagon train had been attacked; six men were dead.

From that time, there was no peace. All through the summer and autumn, soldiers and civilians were slain intermittently. Every tactic of guerrilla warfare in the Indians' repertory—from simple ambush to complicated confusion—was used against the invading whites. Red Cloud even went so far as to teach his braves a few words of English and to dress them in captured blue army uniforms in order to disorganize the soldiers under close attack.

Colonel Carrington obviously did not know what to do. In one communication to headquarters at Omaha, he would urgently request reinforcements; in the next, he would assure his commander that the situation was under control and that there was nothing further to fear from the Indians. He issued innumerable orders to his men; forbidding them to walk on the grass, cau-

Red Cloud. Red Cloud was determined to halt the Army's efforts to keep open the trail across Wyoming to the Montana goldfields. He began his fight in guerrilla fashion, biding his time, waiting for the proper moment to let loose all the might of the various Sioux bands and their Cheyenne allies.

Jim Bridger. One of the shrewdest of the western scouts, Bridger was Carrington's guide and adviser. He disapproved of Fort Phil Kearny's location, but was overruled. In the autumn, Bridger and Bill Williams made a scouting trip through friendly Crow villages. The Crows, hostile to the Sioux, told the scouts that Red Cloud planned to go on the warpath with the coming of snow weather.

tioning against the use of profanity, restricting them to their barracks after tattoo. With all this, an average of a man a day was being scalped or wounded by Indian attacks in the vicinity of the fort.

18

When *Frank Leslie's Illustrated Newspaper* sent out one of its photographer-correspondents, Ridgway Glover, he was carelessly permitted to wander two miles from the gates. The soldiers found his body naked and scalped, his back cleft with a tomahawk.

Carrington issued more orders. No soldiers or civilians would thereafter leave the fort without military authority. No large gates would be opened without special permission. All horses of mounted men must be saddled at reveille.

In order that small details of men might be sent to the timber to fell trees and cut logs, a block house was constructed near the Pinery, seven miles from the fort. Howitzers were frequently used to shell the woods with case shot before the cutters moved in.

Early in the autumn, Carrington sent Jim Bridger and Bill Williams out for a scout among the Indian tribes. While on their reconnaissance, the two veterans of the western trails visited a Crow village at Clark's Fork. The Crows, who had originally claimed all these hunting grounds, still hated the Sioux and looked upon them as interlopers. They readily told Bridger and Williams that Red Cloud and Man-Afraid-of-His-Horses had made visits to the village, asking the Crows to join them on the warpath against the whites. Red Cloud had said that he was only waiting for snow weather; then he would surround the fort, cut off its communications, and starve the soldiers out. He planned two big fights, one at the "Pine Woods" (Fort Phil Kearny), the other at "Big Horn" (Fort C. F. Smith).

On their return, Bridger and Williams warned Carrington to expect an attack by winter. They knew that no matter what Red Cloud's exact strategy might be, the real reason why the Sioux had not already attacked in force was because of lack of organization among the tribes. But during the late summer and early autumn, the various Sioux bands—the Oglalas, Hunkpapas, Brulés, Miniconjous—had been welded together. And with them were most of the Cheyennes and

Arapahoes. When autumn hunts were over and the tribal stores filled for the winter, blood would flow on the snow.

Some historians have discounted Red Cloud's importance in the Indian's war along the Bozeman Trail, pointing out that Man-Afraid-of-His-Horses was the head chief of the Oglalas at that time. However, it is evident that Red Cloud, being the younger and more vigorous man, had won over many of the Sioux as a result of his uncompromising stand against the whites at the Fort Laramie peace council. And he had continued to win followers all through the summer of 1866. Man-Afraid-of-His-Horses was old; the pleasures of hunting were no longer so keen, and the evils of the war were many. To young Red Cloud, the hunting grounds were sacred and inviolable; he would fight to the death rather than see the white man take them.

After the soldiers moved in and started building the fort on the Little Piney, more and more of the Indians came to believe that Red Cloud was right. The white man must be driven from the sacred hunting grounds.

When the Cheyenne chiefs went down to Carrington's tent camp on July 16, a war party of Sioux angrily watched them from afar, suspecting that the Cheyennes were trying to drive a bargain with Carrington against them. As soon as the Cheyennes departed and made camp, the Sioux warriors dashed among them, demanding to know what they were doing in the soldier's camp. When the Cheyennes explained that they wanted to make a peace treaty, the Sioux insulted Black Horse and the other chiefs by striking them across their faces with their bows, and then rode off into the night.

"White man lies and steals," Red Cloud told his followers. "My lodges were many, but now they are few. The white man wants all. The white man must fight, and the Indian will die where his fathers died."

In September, he took personal command of war parties raiding the area around Fort Phil Kearny. His braves used white flags and flashing mirrors for signaling, and the frequency of the attacks increased. When they could not get at the soldiers, they raided wagon trains, stampeding or capturing horses and mules. They heaped hay on Carrington's beloved mowing machines and set them afire, stole most of his beef herd, shot up the herders, sent pursuing soldiers limping and crawling back to the fort with arrows driven into their bodies. They even raided the block house near the Pinery, fired in through the loopholes, scalped one luckless private alive.

The soldiers retaliated with their howitzers, which the Indians respected, calling them "the guns which speak twice." But Carrington realized that his infantrymen were no match for the slippery Indians on their swift-running horses. He called for cavalry, and headquarters sent him one company, which came in piecemeal, from Fort Laramie.

By October 31, the fort was completed, the stockades, warehouses and quarters ready for the winter. Colonel Carrington declared a holiday, issued new uniforms to the entire command, and ordered the men out for a band concert and flag raising. "It is the first full garrison flag that has floated between the Platte and Montana," he told the troops. A poem and a prayer were read, the guns were fired in salute, and the band played "Hail Columbia." Meanwhile, up on Lodge Trail Ridge, appeared red-blanketed Indians riding back and forth on their horses, flashing their mirror signals while they watched the strange celebration below.

A few days later, a young infantry captain joined the Fort Phil Kearny staff. His name was William J. Fetterman, and he had served with some distinction through the Civil War. Fetterman sincerely believed that he knew everything there was to know about fighting, and his contempt for the "untrained" Indian was more than considerable. "Give me a single company of regulars," he boasted, "and I can whip a thousand Indians. With eighty men I could ride through the Sioux nation."

Unfortunately, this reckless bravado was shared by two other officers, Captain Frederick H. Brown and Lieutenant George W. Grummond. Brown often had expressed an intense desire to take Red Cloud's scalp personally.

By December, Red Cloud was ready to give them a chance to make good their boasts and threats. He had won the allegiance of several additional bands of the hesitant Cheyennes, and his total warrior force probably numbered more than two thousand.

Early on the morning of December 6, Red Cloud led his camps up along the Tongue and Prairie Dog Creek, spreading the warriors among the foothills near the fort. Then he sent out a small raiding party, following their movements from a high ridge with a pair of captured field glasses. He was trying to set a decoy trap.

When a wood train moved out from the stockade gate into the pine woods, a small force of shouting Indians surrounded the woodcutters and began attacking. The men signalled back to the fort for help. Operating by a prearranged plan, Colonel Carrington sent Captain Fetterman and Lieutenant H. S. Bingham out towards the wagons with forty mounted men, while the commander with Lieutenant Grummond cut across the Big Piney, hoping to intercept the attackers.

The scheme failed. Bingham and fifteen men became separated from Fetterman near Lodge Trail Ridge, and when the junction was made with Carrington, the Indians had disappeared. Red Cloud's warriors had turned the tables, killing the officer and two of his men.

For the next two weeks, Red Cloud kept large numbers of his warriors moving about the skylines above the fort, and sometimes at night, parties were sent in near the walls, imitating the cries of wolves. One morning, a sentry was found dead inside the fort with an arrow through his chest.

The nerves of the soldiers were on edge. Fetterman went to Carrington and begged for permission to ride out with a company of men and make a bold attack, but the commander refused the request. He chose to watch and wait, hoping for more cavalry reinforcements.

On the twentieth day of December, a large Sioux war party was encamped on Prairie Dog Creek. Here they were joined by their Cheyenne and Arapaho allies, and the ceremonies which always preceded a big battle were begun. A hermaphrodite with a black blanket over his head was sent out to ride a zig-zag path over the low hills. The He-e-man-eh, as he was called, made four rides. Each time, he came back to chant a report that he had caught soldiers in his hands. On his fourth ride, he shouted that he had a hundred soldiers in his hands, and the Sioux warriors cried that this was enough. They beat the ground with their hands, and then the three war parties moved on to Tongue River for a night camp.

The leaders for the coming battle were selected that night, and a young warrior named Crazy Horse was chosen to lead the decoy party. The last time they had failed to trap the soldiers, but this time they would succeed.

At daybreak, they followed the Tongue up to the forks, and here Red Cloud asked the Cheyennes and Arapahoes to choose which side of Lodge Trail Ridge they wished to fight on. The plan was to draw the soldiers down the ridge, with the two forces hidden on either side. The Cheyennes and Arapahoes took the upper side, and the Sioux moved over to their position. Then a large party of picked Sioux warriors set out toward the fort.

Meanwhile, inside the fort the bugler had sounded reveille, and the day's routine had begun. It was only four days until Christmas, and everyone was looking forward to a holiday celebration. The sun shone brightly, and although snow sparkled in the Big Horns, the air was so warm by midmorning that the men working inside the stockade removed their overcoats for comfort.

A lone wood train moved out of the fort, later than

usual that morning, with an extra enforcement of armed guards. About eleven o'clock, the pickets on Pilot Hill began signaling frantically: "Many Indians!" Colonel Carrington was notified, and he stepped outside to join his officers. The women and children also came from their quarters. The next signal informed them that the wood train had gone into corral, and that the Indians were attacking. Carrington turned, quietly giving the order to assemble a relief party immediately. Fifty infantrymen and twenty-seven cavalrymen fell into formation, and two civilians who worked at the post, James Wheatley and Isaac Fisher, volunteered their services. Major J. W. Powell was ordered to command.

But Powell had scarcely mounted his horse before Captain Fetterman stepped forward and asked Carrington's permission to command the party. Fetterman, who had been breveted a lieutenant-colonel for his gallantry in the Civil War, claimed seniority. Carrington hesitated momentarily, then gave Fetterman the command. Lieutenant Grummond had already volunteered to lead the cavalry unit, and Captain Brown, unknown to Carrington, joined the group at the exit gate.

Knowing well the impulsiveness of Fetterman, Carrington tersely warned the captain of the cunning of the Indians waiting in the hills. "Ride direct to the wood train, relieve it, and report back to me. Do not engage or pursue the Indians at the expense of the train. Under no circumstances pursue the Indians over Lodge Trail Ridge."

Captain Fetterman saluted, and turned his horse hurriedly towards the open gate. His mounted men galloped after him, the foot soldiers marching on the double behind them. Carrington strode across the parade ground, mounted a sentry platform, and ordered the troops to halt outside. "Under no circumstances," he repeated to Fetterman, "must you cross Lodge Trail Ridge!" Fetterman acknowledged the order, swung about, and led off at a fast pace down the

24

trail towards the embattled woodchoppers. He was commanding eighty men, exactly the number he had declared he would need "to ride through all the Sioux nation."

Watching from high on the ridge, Red Cloud and the other leaders waited until the soldiers were near the corralled wood train. Then they signaled the attacking force to withdraw. While the tricky warriors around the corral were vanishing into the woods, Crazy Horse and his decoy party were dispatched toward the scene of action.

When Fetterman came in view of the woodchoppers, he saw no Indians, and it appeared to him that they had been frightened away at his approach. His desire to slay the "savages" apparently had been frustrated, and he was angry.

But a few moments later, Crazy Horse on his fast white-footed bay dashed out of the brush, leading his warriors in a zig-zag trail across a slope in front of Fetterman's men. The soldiers opened fire at once. Fearlessly, the decoy party rode in close, whooping

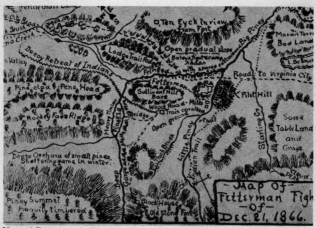

Map of Fetterman's Fight. When a wagon train was attacked by Red Cloud's warriors, Captain William J. Fetterman led the relief party. Warned by Colonel Carrington not to pursue the Indians beyond Lodge Trail Ridge, the rash young officer disobeyed orders and led his command of eighty men directly into an ambush.

25

their blood-chilling yells, waving their blankets to frighten the white men's horses. Then they retreated, always moving jerkily back and forth, slowly, slowly up the slope towards Lodge Trail Ridge, the anger of Fetterman growing as he watched them escaping his riflemen.

The sky had become overcast with gray curdled clouds, and the warmth of the morning had disappeared, the cold deepening as if rising perceptibly from the frozen earth. In the forefront were the cavalrymen, eager to spur their horses onward, while the foot soldiers dug their heels in doggedly to climb the slope and keep closed up. Soon they were past the curving crest of Sullivant Hills, and then they were seen no more by their comrades in the fort.

Ahead of them were the Sioux, the Cheyennes, and the Arapahoes, concealed among the rocks and the brush, waiting silently for the signal to charge. The cavalry moved cautiously now, yards ahead of the panting infantrymen. It was a perfect trap.

Too late Fetterman realized his mistake. As he turned to wave his men back, a hundred "hoka hey's—" shrilled out upon the cold, heavy air, the Sioux surging up out of the earth to smother one flank. The Cheyennes and the Arapahoes were up an instant later. The cavalry swung back bravely against a hilltop and stopped, the walking soldiers taking a position behind a pile of large flat stones. But it was all over in a few minutes.

At first the fighting was hand-to-hand, with war clubs and rifle butts; then the arrows began to fly like rain. The foot soldiers were wiped out, and then the Indians pressed the horsemen back against the steep snow-sheeted hill. It was so cold now that blood froze as it spurted from the wounds. In a final charge, the Indians killed the last man of Fetterman's company. When a dog belonging to one of the soldiers came running out barking, a Sioux shot it through with an arrow. Then the warriors picked up their dead and wounded and rode away.

The incidents which followed the so-called Fetterman Massacre were not entirely anti-climactical. As soon as Colonel Carrington heard the rapid firing from the ambushed soldiers, he sent Captain Tenedore Ten Eyck out with a relief force as large as Fetterman's, but Ten Eyck wisely halted on top of the ridge. He could see literally thousands of Indians moving across the valleys below, and he must have guessed immediately what had happened to Fetterman.

After the Indians had retired from the immediate vicinity of the battle, Ten Eyck's men cautiously retrieved forty-eight of the bodies, returning to the fort with them after dark. By this time, the cold had increased in intensity, with the bleakness that usually precedes a snowstorm.

When a volunteer was requested to ride the two hundred and thirty-five miles to Fort Laramie to obtain reinforcements, a frontier miner offered his services. His name was John "Portugee" Phillips, and his four-day ride through a blinding blizzard, past Indian encampments, with only a few pieces of hardtack in his pocket, is an epic performance in Western history.

At dawn on the twenty-second of December, a council was held in the fort, Carrington surprising his officers with a proposal to search for the remaining bodies. Although the number of men at Fort Phil Kearny was not now sufficient for adequate defense, Carrington declared firmly: "I will not let the Indians entertain a conviction that our dead cannot and will not be rescued. We must not give them an idea of weakness here, which would only stimulate them to risk an assault." He proposed to lead the searching party himself.

Before departing, he opened the power magazine and set the fuses so that all the ammunition could be

Captain William J. Fetterman. His contempt for the "untrained" Indians proved to be his undoing.

Captain Tenedore Ten Eyck. He was sent to rescue Fetterman but arrived too late.

28

Portugee Phillips Arrives at Horse Shoe Station. With the fort surrounded by Indians, the communications cut, and a severe blizzard sweeping deep snows across the trail to the south, Colonel Carrington doubted if any man could get through to bring help. But Phillips rode through the Sioux and the blizzard—a journey that is one of the unsung epics of the West. When he reached Horse Shoe Station, the news of the battle was flashed over the telegraph lines to Fort Laramie.

destroyed by a single match. His order was: "If in my absence, Indians in overwhelming numbers attack, put the women and children in the magazine . . . and in the event of a last desperate struggle, destroy all together, rather than have any captured alive."

But the Indians attacked neither the searching party nor the fort. It is possible that Red Cloud might have stormed the walls with his enormous forces, but for some reason—probably the weather—he chose not to strike. The blizzard that raged until Christmas piled the snow level with the west stockade, and the soldiers had to shovel continuously to keep a protective trench opened.

When reinforcements finally arrived from Fort Laramie, orders also came recalling Colonel Carrington. Captain H. W. Wessels took over the command. Carrington, his staff, his wife and two small sons had to cross Wyoming by wagon train in a continuous blizzard with the temperature as low as 38 degrees below zero.

29

"There never was a more ill-considered impulse of the American people," he said later, "than that which forced the army into the Powder River and Big Horn countries in 1866, to serve the behests of irresponsible, speculative emigration, regardless of the rights of tribes rightfully in possession."

Carrington would spend the remainder of his life trying to justify his actions during his six months' command of the fort on the Little Piney.

III

After his victory over Fetterman, the fame of Red Cloud spread like magic. All the Indians of the Powder River country heralded him as a leader with "big medicine," and as soon as the long cold winter of 1866-67 came to an end, he began making plans to drive the invaders completely from his country.

Unknown to Red Cloud, however, 700 new breech-loading Springfield rifles with 100,000 rounds of ammunition were brought up to the northern forts during the spring. Previously, the soldiers had used the old muzzle-loaders, weapons which the Indians had found scarcely more effective than their deadly arrows. In battle they merely waited until the soldiers delivered their fire, then when they saw the ramrods in use, they would make a wild dash, attacking with arrows and any firearms they might have.

During July, 1867, the Fort Phil Kearny woodchoppers opened full operations in the Pinery several miles from the fort. A small company of soldiers under Major J. W. Powell—whose place Fetterman had taken the day he was slain—was stationed nearby. For defense, Powell had removed the large wooden boxes from the wagon beds and placed them in a rectangular formation.

During the last week of July, Red Cloud gathered his forces together for an attack, but there was considerable disagreement among the chiefs as to the proper place to strike at the white men. Confidence of victory was high among the warriors of all the bands. They had assembled the finest war ponies in the country, and by devious mean had obtained many rifles. But the Cheyennes wanted to attack Fort C. F. Smith, while Red Cloud preferred Phil Kearny, where he had already tasted victory. After the smoking of many pipes and the delivery of long harangues, the final decision was made by a simple process. The warriors were divided into two groups. The chieftains and their bands who wanted to attack the upper fort lined up on one side; those who preferred to attack the other fort formed another line. As there were over five thousand warriors present and as the two forces were almost the same strength, the chiefs decided to attack both forts simultaneously.

The battle at Fort C. F. Smith is now known as the Hayfield Fight, because the soldiers were guarding haycutters outside the fort at the time of the attack. Surrounded inside a barricade of logs and willow boughs, nineteen men successfully fought off hundreds of Indians on August 1, and this assault was a costly failure for the warriors who had not chosen to fight under Red Cloud at Phil Kearny.

Red Cloud, meanwhile, had decided to try his old decoy trick once again, and as before he chose Crazy Horse for the leader. The men stationed outside Fort Phil Kearny under Major Powell offered the easiest target, and Red Cloud decided to slaughter them first, then ambush any relief force that might be sent out from the fort. The night of August 1, wearing their white and green and yellow warpaint, their war bonnets, their feathers in scalp-locks, the warriors moved like dark shadows across the rough country north of the Big Piney.

At dawn they prepared to attack, the decoys moving out into the open. But most of the woodcutters fled back towards the fort, while the remainder with the soldiers—thirty-two men altogether—took their sheltered posts behind the wagon boxes. This time the

The Wagon Box Fight. On August 2, 1867, Red Cloud tried to slaughter a company of woodchoppers who were using a rectangular formation of wagon boxes for defense. But breech-loading rifles had been issued to the soldiers, and the Sioux were forced to retire under the rapid fire of the new weapons. (Painting by Theodore B. Pitman, from a pen sketch by Sgt. Samuel Gibson, who was there.)

Touching the Pen at Fort Laramie. *"From this day forward all wars between the parties to this agreement shall forever cease."*

These words began the treaty drawn up in a large tent at Fort Laramie in April 1868. Old-Man-Afraid-of-His-Horses and Little Wound signed, but Red Cloud and the young hostiles declared they would remain in the Powder River country until the blue-coated soldiers marched away from the forts.

warriors in concealment could not bear to wait for the decoys to lure the men out into the open again. Two hundred sprang out of hiding, stampeding the horses, and then the whole mass of mounted braves began circling the wagon boxes, drawing the noose of the circle tighter and tighter.

But to Red Cloud's consternation the soldiers did not pause between shots to use their ramrods. The screaming bullets spat out continuously and his best warriors went down like grass blades before a blast of wind.

There seemed to be no end to the white men's shooting. Red Cloud signaled the mounted warriors back, and then the Indians tried again, but the same bloody disaster was repeated. For a time there was a pause while the chieftains conferred. In a last charge, almost a thousand warriors who were without horses came swarming up from out of a ravine, while the mounted warriors came in from the other sides. But they could not storm the hail of lead from the new rifles.

When a scout informed Red Cloud that a hundred soldiers were coming from the fort armed with howitzers, he ordered his followers to withdraw. The white man's medicine, this time, had been too strong for him.

For days, Red Cloud thought he had suffered a defeat. In later years, he said he had lost the flower of his fighting warriors and had resolved never to fight again. But back east the news of his resistance had at last made a deep impression upon the officials. The Indian Office reported that the government must either make peace with the Indians north of Powder River or else flood that section of the country with troops and fight a long, costly war.

The government chose to make peace. General William T. Sherman, General William S. Harney, General Alfred H. Terry, General C. C. Auger, J. B. Henderson, Nathaniel G. Taylor, John B. Sanborn and Samuel F. Tappan were appointed commissioners to draw up a treaty. By April, 1868, the terms were

Little Wolf.   When the soldiers at last departed
from Fort Phil Kearny, a band of Cheyennes
under Little Wolf set fire to the buildings.

agreed upon. "From this day forward all war between the parties to this agreement shall forever cease," it began.

The soldiers were withdrawn from Fort C. F. Smith, Fort Phil Kearny and Fort Reno. Before the retiring troops were yet out of sight of Fort Phil Kearny, they looked back and watched a band of Indians under Little Wolf setting fire to the hated buildings.

As for Red Cloud, he now believed that at last he had won back forever the sacred hunting grounds of his people. His illusions would vanish all too soon.

Black Kettle and His Chiefs. This is the only known photograph of Chief Black Kettle of the southern Cheyennes, seated second from left with his sub-chiefs, a pipe in his hand. Black Kettle tried to keep the Cheyennes at peace, and on the advice of the Colorado authorities moved his people into the Big South Bend of Sand Creek near Fort Lyon.

36

2

BLACK KETTLE
OF THE CHEYENNES

WHILE RED CLOUD was still resisting the westward march across Wyoming, another great Indian was striving to settle his differences by diplomatic means. Black Kettle, one of the most famous chiefs of the southern Cheyennes, was the leader of the Colorado tribes whose existence had been menaced by the discovery of gold in that territory.

Black Kettle had tried to keep his people at peace with the invading whites, but in spite of his efforts unavoidable clashes occurred between the Colorado gold miners and the Indians of that region. Upon the advice of Major E. W. Wyncoop, commandant at Fort Lyon, some of the Colorado Cheyennes went to Denver in 1864 to talk with the governor of the territory. As a result of this conference, Black Kettle brought his people to the Big South Bend of Sand Creek, thirty miles northeast of Fort Lyon. To prove his loyalty to the Great White Father, Black Kettle mounted an American flag over his own tipi.

For no apparent reason other than hatred, Colonel J. M. Chivington and his Colorado volunteers attacked this camp in a surprise dawn raid on November 29, 1864. It has been charged that the goldfield volunteers, fearful of being called east to fight in the Civil

Sand Creek Massacre. In a surprise raid on November 29, 1864, Colonel J. M. Chivington and his Colorado Volunteers attacked the peaceful camp of Black Kettle at Sand Creek, killing men, women, and children. Black Kettle saw his wife die, shot down as she tried to flee with him up a dry stream bed.

War, deliberately attempted to foment an Indian war which would keep them at home. Whatever the reason, the indiscriminate slaughter of the surprised Cheyennes was so appalling that some of the most hardbitten frontiersmen were disgusted. Kit Carson, who could scarcely be called a lover of the Indians, described the Sand Creek affair as a cold-blooded massacre. "No one but a coward or a dog would have had a part in it," he said. In the thick of the battle, Black Kettle had seen his wife shot down as she tried to flee up a stream bed.

But as usual, nothing was done by the officials. The Cheyennes and their Arapaho friends were left to take care of themselves, and they did so in the only practicable manner they knew. For weeks, it was not safe for a lone white man to cross a Cheyenne's path in Colorado or western Kansas.

Finally in 1865, Black Kettle was persuaded to sign a new peace treaty. Then when the government almost immediately ignored its guarantees, he lost his prestige with his followers. In 1867, after regaining his supremacy over the southern Cheyenne bands, he tried for the third and last time to make a just peace by negotiation in the famed Medicine Lodge Creek Council in Kansas.

This time Black Kettle and the Cheyennes might have retired to a peaceful existence in the Indian Territory reservation assigned to them, had it not been for the rivalry between various factions in the United States government. Lack of a definite policy in Washington, and a corresponding ascendancy of authority was given the army in the West. The end of the Civil War added to the growth of the army's power in the West, with the release of thousands of officers and soldiers who preferred to serve on the plains rather than return to civilian life.

Among these officers was a dashing young cavalryman, George Armstrong Custer, who came to the West with the cold-blooded intention of making a glorious career out of the business of slaying Indians.

Ever since the closing days of the Civil War, when George Custer was a much-publicized military idol riding up Pennsylvania Avenue in the Grand Army review with his yellow hair flying in the breeze, he had longed for his lost days of glory. He had been reduced from his temporary rank of major general to a mere captaincy, and that seemed to gall him. Even after he worked himself up to the rank of lieutenant-colonel with the Seventh Cavalry, he was irascible, cruel to his men, and was completely barbarous in his relations with the Indians.

Custer had tried to whip the Seventh Cavalry into shape during the desultory campaign under General W. S. Hancock in western Kansas in 1867. But during this period, he more than met his match in the Cheyennes, Arapahoes and Kiowas who resisted all the army's efforts to chase them from the plains. The Indians literally ran circles around him, and Custer took his spite out on his men. He was so unreasonable that many soldiers went AWOL. He ordered them shot without trial, then went AWOL himself in order to visit his wife.

For these military crimes, George Custer was court-martialed in November, 1867. One year later, however, he was back at the head of the Seventh Cavalry again.

After reorganizing the outfit, he decided to win back his prestige and even his score with the Indians simultaneously by some sort of bold stroke. Since he had been unable to best the Indians in open and fair fight on the plains, he planned to surround the peaceful bands in their winter lodges and wipe them out en masse.

In November, 1868, the Seventh Cavalry moved out of Fort Dodge, Kansas, ostensibly "to make the savages live up to their treaty obligations." The "treaty obligations" signed by the Cheyennes, Arapahoes, Kiowas, and Comanches stated that "in case crimes or other violations of law shall be committed by any persons, members of their tribe, such person or per-

Council at Medicine Lodge Creek. Long after Sand Creek, the Cheyennes and their Arapaho allies fought an undeclared war against all settlers and gold miners who crossed their paths. But finally in 1867, Black Kettle was induced to sign a new peace treaty at the famed Medicine Lodge Creek Council in Kansas. The southern Cheyennes and the Arapahoes agreed to retire to a reservation in the Indian Territory.

sons shall, upon complaint being made, in writing, to their agent, Superintendent of Indian Affairs, or other proper authority, by the party injured, and verified by affidavit, be delivered to take such person or persons into custody, to the end that such person or persons may be punished according to the laws of the United States.''

The treaty then specifically stated that ''such hostile acts or depredations shall not be redressed by force or arms.'' This provision was meant to protect innocent Indians from being slain for the crimes of the guilty. Yet it was against the villages of peaceful Indians under Black Kettle that Custer was riding in late autumn of 1868.

General Philip Sheridan agreed with Custer's plans. In fact, he gave the official order: ''To proceed south in the direction of the Antelope Hills, thence toward the Washita River, the supposed winter seat of the hostile tribes; to destroy their villages and ponies; to kill or hang all warriors and bring back all women and children.''

In fairness to the Washington authorities who

41

Kit Carson. The slaughter of the Cheyennes aroused the anger of many frontiersmen, including Kit Carson, who described the Sand Creek affair as a cold-blooded massacre.

George Armstrong Custer. The glories Custer had won in the Civil War were fading, and he was seeking a great victory over the Indians which would bring his name back to the lips of his admirers. After convincing General Philip Sheridan that the Cheyennes and Arapahoes were a menace, Custer received orders to proceed against Black Kettle's lodges.

backed General Sheridan and Lieutenant-Colonel Custer in their action against the Indians along the Washita, it must be made clear that there had been occasional raids, some cattle had been stolen and a few farm houses burned. But these were isolated offenses committed by a few guilty Indians, actions of which most members of the tribes concerned knew nothing. Yet the deeds had been so magnified by distance that in Washington they appeared to be the grossest of crimes.

When Black Kettle and his people went into Fort Larned, Kansas, in July, 1868, to obtain the supplies promised them in exchange for moving on their barren reservation, the authorities refused to give them arms and ammunition necessary for their annual buffalo hunt. This refusal was in direct violation of the Medicine Lodge treaty.

"Our white brothers," said Black Kettle, "are pulling away from us the hand they gave us at Medicine Lodge, but we will try to hold on to it. We hope the Great White Father will take pity on us and let us have the guns and ammunition he promised us so we can go hunt buffalo to keep our families from going hungry."

Finally in August, Black Kettle's old friend of Colorado days, E. W. Wyncoop, now United States Indian Agent at Fort Larned, succeeded in obtaining permission from Washington to give out supplies, including arms and ammunition for the annual buffalo hunt. Soon afterwards, the Cheyennes departed for the autumn hunt, which was very successful. Black Kettle then led his followers, as directed by the government, to a site on the cottonwood-fringed Washita, where they settled down to dry their strips of meat into pemmican, and to dress their buffalo hides into winter garments and lodge coverings. For his own lodge, Black Kettle chose a site under a giant cottonwood at the edge of the camp, where he set up his tipi and displayed his brilliantly colored trophies of the chase. He thought surely that now his people had nothing to worry about all winter; nothing except the ugly rumor

Curing Buffalo Hide. One of the tasks of the western Indian women was stretching and treating the skins of the buffalo. The texture of the buffalo hide was such that it could not be finely dressed, but it was made into heavy clothing for winter, moccasins, and tent covers.

that the Great White Father was planning to move them into a more restricted reserve and make them live in houses and till the soil like white men.

Late in November, Black Kettle, Big Man, Little Rock and some of the other chiefs went to Fort Cobb to talk over this alarming rumor, but they received little consolation. Indeed, they heard further disquieting news. Many soldiers were said to be coming south on a winter campaign. By the time the chiefs returned to the encampment the night of November 26, a blizzard was raging, and if any of the leaders had thought of moving farther south out of range of the approaching army, they would have delayed such action until after the storm had passed.

Custer, however, marched steadily onwards until the sky cleared and moonlight shone bright upon the snow. Meanwhile, his hired Osage scouts brought back the information that Black Kettle's village was directly ahead. There were more women and children than warriors, the scouts said; the Cheyennes' total fighting strength was only about one-fifth that of the soldiers. Custer decided to surround the camp and attack immediately. Certainly now he had a chance to win a "great victory."

At dawn on the morning of November 27, snow blanketed the plains around Black Kettle's village. A film of ice covered the Washita. The old chief must have been filled with foreboding, for he rose earlier than usual that morning and walked out from his lodge to survey the horizon. He was worried about the bad rumor of the soldiers.

If the peaceful winter scene reassured him, his calm was broken a few minutes later by the cries of a squaw running madly down a pony trail just across the narrow river. "Soldiers!" she shouted to her chief.

Undoubtedly the dark memory of Sand Creek must have flashed across Black Kettle's mind, the violent death of his first wife as she ran beside him up the dry stream bed. Would this happen all over again? He ran into his lodge, awakened his young squaw, and picked up his rifle. He then stepped quickly outside and fired off the weapon to alarm the village.

From the nearest lodge, his friend Magpie came hurrying to see what was the matter. It was then that the air was split with the blasting of trumpets signaling a cavalry charge, followed by a few shrill bars of *Garryowen*. Even when bent on a massacre, Custer was a showman, but the muffled drumming of hoofs on the snow soon drowned out the music.

Black Kettle and his squaw had no more than mounted their pony when the cavalrymen charged through the village, firing volleys from carbines and pistols, and slashing at fleeing Indians with their sabers.

Magpie ran back a few steps, watching his beloved chief and the squaw moving away toward the river on

Attack at Dawn. Custer's forces marched through a snowstorm and reached the ice-filmed Washita on the night of November 26, 1868. His Osage scouts informed him that Black Kettle's village was directly ahead—at the site chosen for the Cheyennes by the U. S. government. At dawn Custer ordered the buglers to sound a cavalry charge, and his men swept through the snow-banked lodges, firing carbines and pistols and slashing with sabers.

the pony. But Black Kettle had slumped forward, a bullet burning into his stomach, and another must have hit his shoulders for his arms fell limply as the pony splashed into the shallow river crossing. Unable to aid his chief, Magpie watched him slide into the water, dead, and a moment later his squaw was dead also, the pony fleeing riderless across the drifted snow.

Although Magpie and some of the others escaped, more than a hundred Cheyenne warriors were killed, as well as many women and children never counted. Their tipis were knocked down and heaped into piles with the winter supply of buffalo hides and pemmican. Then everything was burned. Several hundred ponies were also destroyed. All the Indians who were left alive were now captives.

Custer withdrew from the Washita swiftly, fearing

retaliation from the Kiowas and other Cheyenne camps nearby. Major Joel Elliott and a detachment of eighteen men, pursuing the fleeing warriors, had all been surrounded and slain by Indians from some of these neighboring villages, but Custer did not know this at the time of his flight.

The army moved hurriedly north to Camp Supply with the prisoners. There was one very beautiful captive, Monahseetah, the daughter of one of Black Kettle's sub-chiefs who had been killed in the battle.

Magpie. Magpie watched helplessly while Custer's soldiers killed Black Kettle and his squaw as they tried to escape across the river on a pony. But Magpie and a few other warriors escaped to tell the true story of the massacre.

Custer's Prisoners. After Black Kettle and
more than a hundred Cheyenne warriors were
slain, the women captives were rounded up
and herded on foot through bitter cold
weather to the troop's winter base at Camp
Supply.

Custer took such a liking for Monahseetah that he
persuaded General Sheridan to let him keep her with
him as an interpreter, though she neither spoke nor
understood a word of English. When he went back to
Fort Hays four months later to join his wife, Custer, of
course, had to leave Monahseetah behind.

As for the remainder of the southern Cheyennes in
the Indian Territory, they knew they could never,
never again trust the word of the white man or in his
treaties or scraps of paper. And their friends, the
Kiowas and Comanches, knew also. Except for some
of the unyielding Dog Soldier bands, the Cheyennes
were beaten, but the Kiowas and Comanches were
still strong with spirit.

48

Outnumbered by vastly more powerful forces and operating in territory filling rapidly with hostile settlers, the Kiowas and Comanches would wage a continuous guerrilla struggle for almost a decade after Custer's "war to make peace" along the Washita in that winter of 1868-69.

And fittingly enough, it would be the blood brothers of Black Kettle, the Cheyennes in the north, whose might joined with that of the Sioux would finally destroy George Armstrong Custer in the midst of his glory.

Trailing-the-Enemy and His Wife. For a long time after the Battle of the Washita the southern Cheyennes would remain scattered and powerless, broken into small bands, wandering over the southwestern plains. During the battle, however, a visitor from the powerful Kiowa tribe had joined the Cheyennes in the fighting. His name was Trailing-the-Enemy.

50

3

KIOWA AND COMANCHE

I

THE MEDICINE LODGE CREEK council which was held in Kansas in October, 1867, was a marvelous spectacle in which both the uniformed troops of the army and the bedecked warriors of the southern plains performed splendidly. General W. S. Harney marched his soldiers and wagon trains to the meeting place with considerable pomp and ceremony, but the Indians surpassed him by riding up in a swirling formation of five concentric circles, their horses striped with war paint, the riders wearing warbonnets and carrying gay battle streamers. The great swirling wheel of color and motion stopped suddenly at the edge of the soldiers' positions. Then an opening was formed, and the great chiefs waited dramatically and silently for the outnumbered white men to step inside and prove their bravery and good faith.

As splendid a show as it was, however, the Medicine Lodge Treaty accomplished nothing. The government authorities wanted the Indians to retreat to assigned reservations and follow the white man's road. The Indians wanted to be left free to roam the plains and hunt their buffalo. In spite of Black Kettle's best efforts, and the similar hopes of some of the Kiowa and Comanche leaders, no middle ground was possible.

Attending this council were two Indians who would stand out as the great leaders of the southern tribes during the turbulent years ahead, chiefs who would carry on a continuous struggle after peace-loving Black Kettle died on the Washita.

These chiefs were Satanta, the White Bear, of the Kiowas, and Quanah of the Comanches. Both men were merciless killers, but they killed because they knew no other way to keep the lands of their people. They admitted to the Indian commissioners that they were raiding and robbing and scalping. "But the white man lies to us and then steals our lands and kills our buffalo," they would say.

White bear was almost sixty years old at the time of the Council. His body was strong and lithe, but under the hot winds and suns of the southern plains, his face had become creased and blackened like the leather of an old moccasin. He had come to Kansas in his war paint of brilliant red ochre that covered the entire upper part of his body. His tipi, his shield, and his streamers were red also, and he brought with him an old army bugle which he blew on every occasion that presented itself. At one of the meetings with the commissioners, he rode in blowing his bugle and wearing a blue army coat adorned with epaulets that had been presented to him by General Hancock. But the show was almost stolen by another Kiowa chieftan, Kicking Bird, who wore only his native breech clout and a high black silk hat he had begged from Commissioner Alf Taylor.

When the government representatives told White Bear that the Great White Father wanted to provide the Kiowas with comfortable houses upon the richest agricultural lands, the chieftain, who had been resting on his haunches and whittling while he listened to the talk, remained silent for some moments. Then he rose up and replied: "I do not want to settle down in the houses you would build for us. I love to roam over the wild prairie. There I am free and happy. When we sit down, we grow pale and die."

Bonnet and Paint. Indians attending the great Medicine Lodge Council on the Kansas border in 1867 rode up to the meeting place wearing war bonnets and carrying gay battle streamers. (As it appeared in a picture posed later for the Wanamaker Collection.)

At the time of the final reading of the treaty, many of the chiefs signed, but some did not. Among the Kiowas, only Kicking Bird was sincere when, after listening to the words of the agreement, he said that he would try to follow the white man's road. Lone Wolf refused to sign. White Bear in all his kaleidoscopic glory stepped forward and made his mark on the paper, but he had no intention of obeying the provisions of the treaty. He had already declared himself otherwise.

Among the Comanches, there was much disputation about the treaty. Ten Bears, the old Yamparika Comanche, had spoken plainly. "I was born upon the prairie," he said, "where the wind blew free and there was nothing to break the light of the sun. I was born where there were no enclosures and where everything drew a free breath. I want to die there and not within walls." But he added that he wanted "no blood upon my land to stain the grass," and he urged all the Comanches to sign the treaty.

Quanah, the leader of the Kwahadi Comanches, however, would listen to none of this talk. Quanah, the half-breed son of a chief and a captured white girl, Cynthia Ann Parker, could see no good in a treaty that would take away from his people their freedom of the range. And so this warlike Kwahadi of the Texas Panhandle left the Council before the day of the signing, saying to the other Indians as he departed: "I am not going to a reservation. Tell the white chiefs when they ask, that the Kwahadis are warriors and that we are not afraid."

Little more than a year after this much-publicized "peace" council, Sheridan and Custer were destroying the villages of the Kiowas and Cheyennes all along the Washita River. After the slaughter of Black Kettle's Cheyenne band, the Kiowa chiefs decided to move their people to the Fort Cobb agency. As it was mid-winter, and the soldiers had left them no food, clothing, or shelter, there was no other choice.

To arrange the surrender, White Bear and Lone

Wolf approached Sheridan's camp, bearing white flags. Custer went out to meet them, and he was so unfriendly that some of the other Kiowas leaders, who were waiting nearby, ran away and led their bands into hiding places to the southwest. White Bear and Lone Wolf undoubtedly would have departed also, but Custer put them under guard and told them they would be kept as hostages until the Kiowas came in to Fort Cobb. White Bear's son was sent to carry the message back to the other chieftains.

The Kiowas, hiding in the woods, replied that they would come in as soon as their chiefs were released. When he heard this, General Sheridan lost his temper. He informed White Bear that he would hang him and Lone Wolf to the nearest tree at sunrise if their people did not appear in camp by that time. White Bear conferred with his son, who immediately jumped on his horse and rode away. The old chief looked calmly at the general. "When the sun is there," he said, indicating the western horizon, "the tribe will be here."

And so the Kiowas came in to take the white man's road, all of them except the small bands of Kicking Bird and Woman Heart, who fled to the Staked Plains to join the free Kwahadis.

The white man's road, however, was not easy for these hunters of the plains who heretofore had known no boundaries of time or space. The younger warriors slipped away from the reservation on the slightest pretexts, and in the autumns, the call of the buffalo hunt was too strong even for the older and wiser ones. Although the government had established Fort Sill in the middle of the Kiowas' reserve in 1869, the soldiers could not keep their charges confined, and as soon as the Indians were outside the limits, they inevitably came into violent conflict with the white settlers.

In the spring of 1871, White Bear himself led a raid into Texas. He had heard that the white men were planning to build a railroad across his old hunting grounds, and he could not stand for that. With about a hundred warriors he rode across the familiar prairie,

White Bear.   Most powerful of the tribes at Medicine Lodge were the Kiowas, and their principal chief was Satanta, the White Bear. He arrived in war paint of brilliant red ochre, carrying a battered army bugle which he blew on every possible occasion. White Bear signed the treaty but did not expect any good to come of going on a reservation.

56

looking for any travelers who might be trespassing there. An unlucky wagon train was surrounded, and seven teamsters were killed before White Bear blew his bugle and called off his braves.

When he returned to the reservation, White Bear was summoned before General William T Sherman who had come out from Washington to see the Indian problem at first hand. Sherman was sitting on an open veranda just outside two large windows when White Bear and three other chieftains, Lone Wolf, Sitting Bear, and Big Tree, approached him. Although the sun was intensely hot, the four Indians were wearing heavy blankets.

"Why did you go down into Texas and murder those helpless teamsters who didn't know how to fight?" Sherman asked them directly. "If you want a fight, the soldiers here can always accommodate you."

If White Bear was surprised to learn that Sherman knew all about the raid, he did not betray any evidence on his weather-beaten face. He said that he had heard the Texans were about to build a railroad down there, and he could not permit that. "The road would frighten the buffalo away," he added.

Sherman did not waste words. He told the Kiowas that they were all under arrest and would be sent back to Texas and tried for murder. Upon hearing this remark, Lone Wolf threw off his blanket, cocked his previously concealed carbine, and looked defiantly at Sherman. White Bear and the other two chieftains followed his example, but the window shutters behind the general flew open immediately, and the muzzles of two dozen rifles covered the Indians. In the confusion, Lone Wolf managed to escape, but White Bear, Sitting Bear and Big Tree were caught in Sherman's well-laid trap.

On the way back to Texas for the trial, Sitting Bear was killed while trying to escape. White Bear and Big Tree were tried and sentenced to death, but on the advice of the Indian agents, who feared a general up-

Surrender. The Medicine Lodge Creek Council was a failure, as Custer's attack on Black Kettle's village soon demonstrated. After the slaughter of the Cheyennes, White Bear and Lone Wolf of the Kiowas decided to save their people from similar destruction by surrendering to the army. (The meeting with Custer. *Left to right:* Little Heart, Lone Wolf, Kicking Bird, White Bear, Scout Amos Grover, George Custer, Tom Custer, and J. Schuyler Crosby.)

Fort Sill, 1871 Fort Sill was established in the middle of the Kiowas' reserve in 1869, but the soldiers could not keep the freedom-loving buffalo hunters confined. Hearing that the government planned to build a railroad across the Kiowa hunting grounds, White Bear and Big Tree led a hundred warriors on a raiding party along the proposed route.

rising if the chiefs were hanged, the sentence was commuted to life imprisonment.

But even so, the Kiowas wanted White Bear released. They began a series of retaliatory raids. Kicking Bird, who had returned from the Staked Plains and had been sincerely working for peace, told the officials that the trouble would increase if White Bear were not released. Lone Wolf said the same thing. White Horse declared that his band would continue raiding until White Bear was free, and when nothing was done immediately, he and Lone Wolf visited the Cheyennes and tried to persuade them to join in a big war against all the white men.

Finally in October, 1873, the tired old chieftain and his friend, Big Tree, were released from jail and brought back to Fort Sill. Thomas Battey, the new Indian agent, said that the joy of White Bear and his people was "exhibited in a most wild and natural manner."

But the joy was not to endure. At the first report of a raid in Texas, the local authorities and the press blamed White Bear and Big Tree. In November, 1874, General Sheridan ordered the two leaders arrested and sent to prison at Huntsville, Texas. Agent Battey declared: "To my certain knowledge Big Tree was at home, sick in his lodge, and White Bear was enjoying, after two years' confinement in prison, the pleasures of the buffalo chase on territory assigned for that purpose." The authorities could not find Big Tree, but White Bear was captured and put back into a convict's striped uniform.

Now the old Kiowa was trapped for good. He lived two years, sprawling morosely on the floor of his cell, or standing for hours gazing out the window. In the autumn of 1876, at the time of the annual buffalo hunt, he cut the arteries of his neck and legs. When the white men tried to keep him from dying by taking him to the prison hospital, he grimly outwitted them by leaping out a second-story window. This time he was dead.

Lone Wolf. Arrested by General Sherman after going on a raid with White Bear into Texas, Lone Wolf drew a concealed carbine from his blankets and escaped.

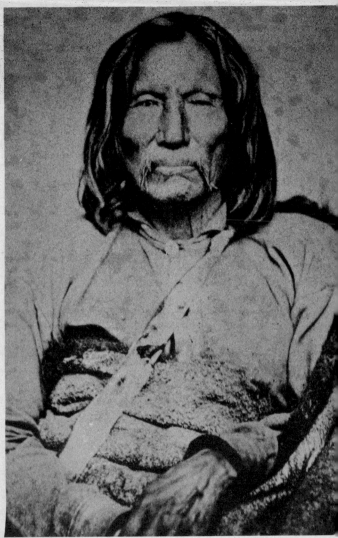

Sitting Bear. On the way to Texas with White Bear and Big Tree, old Sitting Bear was killed while trying to escape. After singing the death song of the soldier society to which he belonged, he slipped his handcuffs loose and seized a carbine from one of the guards. In the resulting struggle, the old Kiowa's body was riddled with bullets.

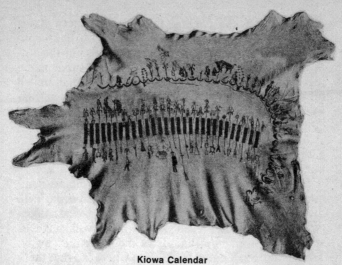

Kiowa Calendar

The old buffalo days of the Kiowas were coming to an end. On this calendar drawn by Anko, a member of the tribe, the outstanding occurrences of the latter days are told in pictures. These figures were drawn in brilliant colors, and only the calendars of the Sioux rival this one in beauty and originality of design.

II

News of the Kiowas and their troubles came occasionally to the camps of the Kwahadi Comanches far to the west. Eagle Heart, White Horse, Woman Heart and other Kiowa chieftains had taken their bands into the Staked Plains, and they had become strong friends of the Comanches.

When evil days fell upon White Bear and his people, Quanah, the Kwahadi chief, resolved more strongly than ever to avoid the white men. The Comanches, he said, would never go on a reservation as the Kiowas had done.

Yet the white men kept coming from the east. The buffalo hunters came by tens and by hundreds, and it seemed that all would be lost. Finally in the spring of 1874, Quanah realized that his people must make a great decision. All the Indians of the southern plains would have to join forces and fight with their concerted might against the buffalo hunters and the settlers, or else all the Indians would have to move on the reservations and live like white men. Quanah called for a great council of the Comanches, and invited their friends who were still free among the Kiowas and Cheyennes.

And so from all over the vast plains, the Indians gathered together to hold a medicine dance near the mouth of Elk Creek on the North Fork of Red River.

During the dance, the Kwahadis' medicine man, Isatai, convinced Quanah that he had conversed with the Great Spirit. "The Great Spirit has at last taken pity on the people," said Isatai. "He will make us strong in war and we shall drive the white men away. The buffalo shall come back everywhere, so that there shall be feasting and plenty in the lodges. The Great Spirit has taught me strong medicine which will turn away the white man's bullets."

Quanah was not too certain of Isatai's power, but he permitted him to make a ceremony at the final feast. When Quanah saw that the other chiefs wanted to believe in Isatai, he presented them with a plan of attack. "First we will drive out the buffalo hunters," said Quanah.

Lone Wolf of the Kiowas disagreed. He wanted to raid the reservations and kill the agents and the soldiers. "If Isatai's power is strong," he said, "we shall have nothing to fear from the soldiers." Stone Calf of the Cheyennes, however, was more practical and thought it best to attack the small isolated groups of buffalo hunters. The Great Spirit might be displeased if they asked for too much help from him all at once.

At last the decision was made. Quanah would make the plan and lead the Comanches. Isatai would make the strong medicine. Lone Wolf and Stone Calf would lead the Kiowa and Cheyenne warriors.

Quanah's plan was simple. They would attack the southernmost of the buffalo hunters' camps at Adobe

Walls in the Panhandle country. After disposing of the hunters there, they would move northward to the next camp, the next, and then the next, always moving more swiftly than the news of the killings, until they had destroyed all the invaders of the buffalo country.

Before dawn of June 27, seven hundred warriors rode up out of the shadows of the Canadian River valley and spread themselves along the edge of the timber of Adobe Walls Creek. Quanah, in the lead, could see only the smudgy outlines of the buildings of Adobe Walls, picketed and built stockade fashion —two stores, a saloon, and a blacksmith shop. The thirty hunters, who had come to slay the Indians' buffalo and leave the skinned carcasses rotting on the plains, were all asleep.

And so they would have remained asleep had not a drying ridge pole over one of the sheds happened to crack loudly just before daylight. The sharp noise awakened Billy Dixon, the famous Texas scout. Once awakened, Dixon was in no mood to go to bed again. As he walked towards his horse, he saw the animal fling its head back and prick up its ears. Billy Dixon whirled around.

Across the valley in the graying dawn, hundreds of mounted Indians in their war paint, feathers, and other trappings of battle, were sweeping towards the trading post. Dixon had barely enough time to awaken his companions before the first war whoops shrilled out above the drumming hoofs. The noise of the breaking ridge pole had probably saved their lives.

The story of the battle of Adobe Walls is only another version of Red Cloud's Wagon Box fight. This time instead of breech-loading rifles, the buffalo hunters possessed new long-range weapons. Although Quanah led his warriors in charge after charge, sometimes to the point of beating upon the doors of the stockade with their rifle butts, they could never break into the trading post. The siege continued throughout the day. When the horse of Isatai, the medicine man, was shot from under him, he blamed the failure of his

Quanah Parker. Leader of the Kwahadi
Comanches, Quanah was the son of a chief
and a captured white girl, Cynthia Ann Parker.
When he saw what was happening to the
Kiowas, he resolved to drive all the settlers
off the Staked Plains. But in a bloody fight at
Adobe Walls in June 1874, he and his Kiowa
and Cheyenne allies suffered the same fate as
Red Cloud in the Wagon Box fight, for the
buffalo hunters now had long-range weapons.

power on a Kiowa brave who had recently killed a rabbit without his permission.

Quanah kept the battle going at intervals for three days, and then he knew he was beaten. He had been wounded in the shoulder, his best warriors were dead or injured, the news of the attack had already been spread to the north by passing hunters. And worst of all, the power of Isatai had failed.

Even if Adobe Walls had not proved to Quanah that the fate of the southern plains Indians was already sealed, the events of the succeeding weeks certainly must have done so. From Camp Supply, General Nelson Miles was leading an army column toward the Kwahadi country. Colonel Ranald S. Mackenzie was marching from Fort Griffin in Texas. A third column was operating from Fort Sill. And even from the west, a small force was ready to strike eastward out of Fort Union, New Mexico.

The day of the buffalo was over for the Comanches. The wild, free days were ended for all the Indians of Oklahoma and Texas. They could choose either to die or to take the white man's road.

Quanah chose the white man's road. He led the Kwahadis in to their reservation and then went to visit the white relatives of his mother, Cynthia Ann Parker. "If she could learn the ways of the Indians," he said, "I can learn the ways of the white man." And the Parkers helped him in his long struggle.

He now called himself Quanah Parker. As the years went by, he became a shrewd business man, built a large house, and successfully managed his farm and ranch. He traveled all over the country, and went to Washington to ride in President Theodore Roosevelt's inaugural parade. After long years of effort, he finally achieved something that few other chiefs had ever dreamed of—full American citizenship for all the members of his tribe. The old fighting Kwahadi had come a long way down the white man's road.

Wife of Cochise. Constant warfare developed great leaders among the Apaches. Cochise, chief of the Chiricahuas, was the greatest of the warriors, and even greater as a diplomat. Over six feet tall, a strong and wise leader of a fierce people, it was inevitable that Cochise should clash with the white intruders. His photograph was never taken. His wife was not so adamant.

4

THE CONQUEST OF COCHISE

I

SOUTH AND WEST of the home of Satanta and Quanah Parker the land wore a different face. Here the sun rose and set on rocky peaks, separated by steep gorges. Ashes from a thousand sleeping volcanoes struggled with the life of the land. Here water was hidden; springs and rivers few. Trails were dim and led through country that even a mule found difficult.

Wood, water, and grass, necessary trinity of the westward-pushing white man, were scarce. The few fertile valleys were oases, yielding deer, bear, and wild fowl in abundance.

Such a land was not made to be coveted by the white man. Nevertheless, he pushed in, first from the south into Chihuahua and Sonora, and later from East and West alike. The few green valleys of this desert became the goal of fortune seekers, and life-giving springs became way stations on trails, or sites for military posts. The barren hills were ransacked for gold; the valleys became cattle ranges.

Resisting the push of the white man was the Apache Indian, Ishmaelite of this desert. He was a true son of his pitiless environment: cruel, cautious, crafty, cunning. Thievery was his trade, and death his trademark. The blackrobed fathers who had peacefully conquered

Apache Rancheria. The Apache Indian,
native of Arizona and New Mexico, withstood
the intrusion of the white man as best he
knew. Bows and arrows were soon replaced
with guns, and the Apache became the
equal—in fact, the superior—of his white foe.
For the ways of the Indian were the ways of
the land; each rock was a fortress, and every
canyon an ambush place.

other southwestern tribes found the Apaches unrepentant and exceedingly skillful sinners.

In the early days, before the gold fever drew men a thousand miles in madness, the Apache, armed with bows and arrows, was not a factor to draw attention in the annual reports of the War Department in Washington. Captain John Pope derided them as sneak thieves who were never known to attack more than ten men at a time.

But as the white man trespassed more deeply and permanently into the homeland of this desert people, and when muskets or breech-loading rifles were placed into hands eager and able to use them, the Apaches ranked with the Comanches as the scourge of the southwest. Intermittent wars flared for half a century. The names of warriors and soldiers—Cochise, Mangas Coloradas, Geronimo, Nachez, Victorio, Crook, Carleton, Gatewood, Miles—are still written in the land of Arizona and New Mexico.

It was the time of the Civil War. The whites were shooting each other; a very good time for the Apaches to re-establish their right to the land. White interlopers were robbed and killed. Both Union and Confederate forces were attacked. The helpless citizens abandoned their claims and crowded together in Tucson, Tubac and various ranches.

Chief enemy of the Apaches during this period was Colonel James Carleton, who organized the California Column and fought the Apaches for four years. At the end of that time, the great chief Mangas Coloradas was dead, treacherously shot "while escaping arrest". But Cochise, strong, six-foot chief of the Chiricahua Apaches, greater as a warrior, and yet greater as a diplomat, was left to defend his land.

Cochise had a special hatred for the white man. In 1861, he was accused of stealing a small boy from a ranch near Fort Buchanan. The boy, later known as Mickey Free, had been kidnapped by Pinal Apaches. Lt. George Bascom, Seventh Cavalry, camped near Apache Pass, was determined to make Cochise return the boy. When Cochise came to Bascom's tent for a talk, the soldiers tried to capture him. The fighting chief drew a knife, and ripped his way to freedom through the rear of the tent. His companions were seized as hostages.

Cochise gathered his followers and proceeded to capture several white men to assure the safe return of Bascom's prisoners. The exchange was never made, and Cochise rode away to kill the whites he had taken. In retaliation, three Indian hostages were hanged.

Cochise became implacable. "I was at peace with the whites," he said, "until they tried to kill me for what other Indians did; now I live and die at war with them." In his war, he is known to have burned thirteen white men alive, tortured five to death by cutting small pieces from their feet, and dragged fifteen to death at the end of a lariat.

The chief made war with all the energy of his nature, but he made peace, too, when it suited his purpose. In September, 1871, he consented to meet General Gordon Granger at the Indian agency at Canada Alamosa. He would hear what the white man had to offer, but he would not forget the dismal end of Mangas Coloradas.

General Granger nervously smoked a pipe of peace with the chief, and then quickly spoke. The Great White Father, he said, wanted to live in peace with his red children. He would give Cochise mountains and valleys in Tularosa as a reservation, a home for him and his children forever. In return, the Apaches must remain at peace, steal no stock, raid no settlements, and permit the white man to take over the rest of the country unopposed.

Cochise and his followers retired to consider the words of the General. The chief returned to reply with fierce dignity. "When I was young I wandered all over this country, east and west, and saw no other people than the Apaches. After many summers I walked again, and found another race of people had come to take it. How is it? I will not lie to you; do not lie to me. I want to live in these mountains. I do not want to go

Mickey Free. In 1861, Mickey Free, a white boy, was kidnapped by Pinal Apaches. He later became a government scout and interpreter. His left eye had been gouged out by a deer, but he was a sharp trailer with his one eye. Al Sieber, chief of scouts, described Mickey as "half Irish, half Mexican, and whole son-of-a-bitch."

Apaches Ready for Fight. A mountain people, the Apaches developed large chests and great lungs, giving them staying powers beyond those of their enemies. Fighting and running was the Apache way of making war, a method that kept the white man busy for fifty years.

73

to Tularosa. That is a long ways off. The flies on those mountains eat out the eyes of the horses. The bad spirits live there. I have drunk of these waters and they have cooled me; I do not want to leave here."

A few months later, the Apaches at Canada Alamosa were removed to Tularosa valley in the Mogollon mountains; Cochise and his warriors went back to his home in southern Arizona.

Other Apaches who sought peace left their *rancherias* in the wilds and came in to the army camps for protection. In February, 1871, Eskiminzin, chief of the Arivaipa Apaches, with one hundred and fifty followers came to Camp Grant. They were poor, they said, and hungry, tired of being hunted and killed. They wanted a place to live in peace. Lt. Royal E. Whitman, commander at Camp Grant, believed them, and gave them a place near the post on land which had once belonged to the Apaches.

The settlers in nearby Tucson were alarmed. Almost daily they spoke of Indian raids in the vicinity. Eskiminzin and his warriors were blamed. The citizens, when the army did not take their point of view, decided to act themselves. On April 28, 1871, a party of six Americans, forty-eight Mexicans and ninety-two Papago Indians gathered in Pantano Wash, east of Tucson.

Early in the morning of April 30, the mob, armed by the Adjutant-General of Arizona Territory, attacked the unsuspecting camp of Arivaipas. Most of the warriors, including the chief, were off in the mountains, hunting. Squaws, old men, and children were left to be massacred. In a few minutes one hundred eight of these helpless ones were killed. Twenty-nine children were taken captive and sold as slaves, or kept as servants by residents of Tucson.

Participants in the massacre were later tried in Tucson and acquitted. To murder an Indian was no crime.

Eskiminzin, His Son and Daughter. Eskiminzin, chief of the Arivaipa Apaches, did not want to fight. He sought protection at Camp Grant, near Tucson, Arizona. The citizens of the town formed a mob and attacked the Apache camp, massacring the women, old men, and children. The chief and his warriors, who were out on a hunt, escaped.

75

White Intruder. Hearing of the Camp Grant massacre, other Apache tribes commenced making war with new vigor. Among their victims was Fred W. Loring of Boston, who accompanied Lieutenant George Wheeler's survey expedition as correspondent for *Appleton's Journal*. (The picture of Loring and his mule, ''Evil Merodach,'' was taken about four hours before his death, November 5, 1871.)

On Christmas Day, 1872, Companies L and M, Fifth Cavalry, commanded by Major William H. Brown, accompanied by a detachment of thirty Apache scouts, plodded through the Superstition Mountains of central Arizona. It was a poor holiday. The mountain heights were snow-covered, and cold, wet winds chilled the slopes. What fires were permitted were small, hardly enough to warm the hands, or dry a pair of moccasins.

During the day, Company G of the same regiment, out from Fort McDowell with a party of one hundred Pima Indians, joined Major Brown's command. The combined parties were in the heart of hostile Apache country, and looking for a fight. The native scouts, under half-breed Archie MacIntosh, worked far ahead of the command looking for the Apache *rancheria* supposed to be hidden in the mountain range known as Matitzal, or Four Peaks. Somewhere in those wilds was the camp of Delche, notorious anti-reservation chief.

Only two men of the combined party knew where they were going, Major Brown and an Apache scout, Nantaje, known to the soldiers as Joe. Nantaje had been raised in the Matitzal, and knew the hiding places of his people. He would lead the white men there.

On the evening of December 27, camped in the canyon of Cottonwood creek, just at the eastern foot of Four Peaks, Major Brown told his officers of his plan. There was a cave, he explained, in the canyon of the Salado or Salt River. Here the Apaches were supposed to be hidden. The command was going to surround and surprise the place, and deal a crippling blow to Indian power.

All precautions for surprise were taken. The white soldiers, learning from the Indian scouts, wore moccasins, and stuffed them with dry grass. With such footwear they could walk softly; the rocks would not betray them. Pack mules and surplus equipment were left behind, under guard. Guns and ammunition were all that was necessary for the business at hand. Bacon, bread, and a little coffee were taken by each man, and a canteen of water hung on each belt. The Apache scouts skinned a mule and feasted in anticipation of the fight.

The approach to the cave began when darkness hid the movements of the men. Silently the fighters followed the lead of Nantaje, who assured them they were close to the cave and would soon find plenty of Indians. The route took them up the steeps of the Matitzal to the canyon of the Salado, and on the high mesa which bordered it. Fresh Indian tracks were found, and Company G under Lt. James Burns was dispatched to follow.

Just before dawn Nantaje and MacIntosh led Lt. William J. Ross with half a dozen of the best shots along a rough trail down the canyon of the Salado. It was dangerous work. A slip meant death on the rocks hundreds of feet below. A sudden turn in the angle of the wall revealed the promised cave, in reality a shelf of the great canyon wall, protected on all sides by great, smooth boulders, splintered off the cliff.

A party of Apaches, just back from a raid, were hunched about a small fire. The attackers took aim; each man chose his target silhouetted against the dancing flames. The roar of rifles echoed from canyon walls, and was answered by yells of surprise and hatred within the cave. A few scattered arrows were sent in the general direction of the attack, but Ross and his men were safe, each behind a rock. A quick rush past the cave lodged men on the other side, and the Indians were trapped.

Major Brown called on the Apaches to surrender. The answer was a volley of bullets and arrows, sped with screams of defiance. The Apaches were ready to die. The soldiers directed their shots against the roof of the cave, and the ricochet caught the huddled in-

Apache Scouts. Warriors from among the reservation Apaches were enlisted as scouts to track down their people in their hiding places. The scouts were wild and unmilitary, but highly efficient and trustworthy.

The Head Delivered. Rewards were offered for heads of the important hostile chiefs. Delche, a great fighter, had an especially high price on his head. It was brought in several times—a different head each time—and the reward was always paid.

mates. Cries of wounded, and wails of frightened children indicated that the indirect fire was effective.

Suddenly a death chant began. It spoke of revenge and despair. A charge followed, driven back with bloody losses, but the death chant continued, punctuated by constant fire against the roof of the cave.

On the rim of the canyon, above the cave, death loomed in a new form. Lt. Burns and G Company heard the roar of the fight, and watched proceedings from above. They decided to roll rocks over the cliff onto the shelf. Destruction fell on the Apaches with a crash. Screams of the dying pierced the dust, rising high in the air. Only echoes responded. The death chant was quiet. No rifle spoke. The cave was the house of the dead.

Sixty-six Apaches died in the battle of Salt Canyon, and the one warrior who escaped alive was killed soon after at Turret Butte, another supposedly impregnable Indian refuge.

The fight in the canyon of the Salado was but one of many which were being forced on the Apaches by a new enemy, General George Crook. He had come from Indian campaigns in Oregon and Idaho. The "Grey Wolf," as the Apaches learned to call Crook, had sent white soldiers from every camp in Arizona with instructions to stay in the field until they had located and subdued the last Apache. Pack mules were equipped and trained as support to these columns, and friendly Indians led the white soldiers to the hiding places of their people.

Warfare such as this was too much, even for the Apaches. Peace on the reservations was better. When Crook sent captives out with the news that surrender would be accepted, all the Indians within reach came in. On April 27, 1873, the last of the Apaches surrendered at Camp Verde. Chalipun, Apache-Mohave chief, approached the General and explained his surrender. "You see, we are nearly dead from want of food and exposure—the copper cartridge has done the business for us. I am glad of the opportunity to surrender, but I do it not because I am afraid of the General.''

Old Delche came in, too. He had boasted one hundred twenty-five warriors six months before; twenty were left. "There was a time," he complained, "when we could escape the white soldiers. But now the very rocks have become soft. We cannot put our feet anywhere. We cannot sleep, for if a coyote or fox barks, or a stone moves we are up—the soldiers have come."

General Crook was not only a fighter, but a human being as well. He became the best friend the Apaches ever had. Under his stern but understanding rule, the Apaches settled on reservations and tried to walk the white man's road. They no longer roamed freely over the mountains, but they could rest at night, and live in peace. They tried to forget the old ways, and learn to raise corn instead of scalps.

Issue Day, San Carlos. Rations were issued to the Indians at the agencies to make up for food which could not be raised or hunted. Apache wars stopped, for a while.

Staking Down Buffalo Skins, 1870. There was plenty of buffalo meat for pemmican and skins for new lodges in the Powder River country. Here Red Cloud and his people lived after the peace treaty of 1868. Their horses grew many and fat; life was good.

5

TREATIES AND THE THIEVES' ROAD

I

AFTER RED CLOUD touched the pen in 1868, he and his band went up to the Powder River country. Here they found life as it had been. There was plenty of buffalo for the lodges. The squaws were busy drying meat, making robes, and serving their men. The horses grew fat on the good grass, undisturbed by white men. The forts were burned, and the soldiers had gone away.

Spotted Tail stayed near the Missouri, closer to the agency, above Fort Randall. But he, too, had seen enough of the whites. Their whisky and diseases seemed to come up the river on every steamboat. Spotted Tail kept his people far enough away from the agency to dilute the traders' poison. He was content to draw rations and live in peace according to the terms of the treaty.

In the summer of 1870, Red Cloud with seventeen head men and three squaws, and Spotted Tail with four Brulé chiefs, were taken to Washington for a talk. On their way east they would see how many white people there were, and realize that it was useless to object to whatever might be proposed.

The opportunity to impress the chiefs was not

Red Cloud's Head Men. En route to Washington in the summer of 1870, Red Cloud and other chiefs stopped at Omaha, where photographs were taken. (*Left to right, seated:* Sitting Bull, Swift Bear, Spotted Tail; *standing:* Julius Meyer (interpreter), Red Cloud.)

84

wasted. Red Cloud was told that he should move on a reservation, near an agency, like Spotted Tail, preferably on the Missouri. The chief was obstinate. "The white children have surrounded me, and left me nothing but an island. When we first had this land we were strong, but now are melting like snow on a hillside, while you are grown like spring grass. I have two mountains in that country, the Black Hills and the Big Horn mountains. I want the father to make no roads through them. I have told these things three times, and now have come here to tell them the fourth time. I do not want my reservation on the Missouri."

The treaty of 1868 was then explained to Red Cloud. For the first time, he knew the truth of what had been done. It was as the white man had boasted, "The chiefs have sold themselves for another feast of crackers and molasses."

Red Cloud spoke in anger, now. "You whites have a chief to go by, but the only chief I go by is God Almighty. The whites think the Great Spirit has nothing to do with us, but he has. After fooling with us and taking away our property they will have to suffer for it hereafter."

When Red Cloud returned to his people, they knew his spirit had been bowed. It was whispered in the lodges that he had allowed the whites to capture his spirit in the black image box, the camera. The chief left the Powder River country in July, 1871, and settled near the new agency by Fort Laramie. Spotted Tail also went to a new place on upper White River.

But there were still many Sioux who scorned the example of Red Cloud and Spotted Tail. They refused to move on the white man's island. It was better to hunt buffalo on the Powder than eat wormy pork from the agency. Some of the people who went to the agency in winter always came away again at the time of the new grass. Crazy Horse, Black Moon, and Sitting Bull defied the treaties. Was not this land theirs? Had they not wrested it from the Crows fifty years before, and lived in it, and defended it ever since?

Old Bull.   Old Bull, a Brulé Sioux, was one of many warriors who refused to follow Red Cloud to the reservation. He, with Crazy Horse, Sitting Bull and others, stayed on the prairie with the buffalo, the land, and the sky.

Hayden Survey Party, 1870.   The good buffalo country in the Powder River region was invaded in the early 1870s by surveyors, who came ahead of the railroad. It meant the end of the last great Sioux hunting ground.

They had even driven the white man from it a short while ago.

The government let these wild ones alone until 1871, when surveyors for the railroad began measuring the hills. This was bad medicine. Where these strange whites came, other always followed. The surveyors pushed through the heart of the good buffalo land, through the hunting grounds of the Sioux, the Cheyennes, and northern Arapahoes. The Indians struck back.

Surveyors were attacked. Black Moon with several hundred Sioux and Cheyennes attacked eight troops of cavalry under Major E. M. Baker near Pryor's Fork, Montana, on August 14, 1872. Before the year ended, there were five more big fights against trespassers in that country. The Sioux and Cheyennes found that the words of the peace commissioners were hollow.

There was little the warriors could do. They could swoop down, now and then, on the men who were building the iron road, but the soldiers were always on guard. Five times the warriors gathered and attacked Fort Abraham Lincoln near Bismarck. But the old days of victory were gone. The white soldiers had too many guns, and even artillery.

Some of the Black Kettle Cheyennes were with Crazy Horse, and from them he learned that among the soldier chiefs in Dakota was one called Custer, the squaw-killer. He had been sent from the south to do his work among the Sioux. Crazy Horse attacked Custer on the Yellowstone, August 11, 1873. But it was as a flea bite to a charging white bear.

General Sheridan, in command of the Division of the Missouri, believed that a fort in the Black Hills would make it easier to protect the advance of the railroad. In July, 1874, he sent a reconnaissance expedition to the Hills under Colonel Custer. The report of this scout, published August 12, 1874, meant the death of the treaty of 1868. Gold— "from the grassroots down"—was what Custer found.

The expedition had broken the very words of the

87

Custer's Camp, Hidden Wood Creek, 1874. A reconnaissance expedition under Colonel George A. Custer was sent to the Black Hills, sacred hunting ground and medicine country of the Sioux. Here, the whites believed, would be a good place for another fort. What Custer found was gold.

treaty; the law books said that Indian lands would never be violated, but gold was reported, and the magic sound brought the whites on a run. The "Thieves' Road," as Fast Bear called Custer's trail, was soon worn deep by fortune hunters.

Now that the Black Hills looked good to the white man, it was time for another treaty. A seven-man commission headed by Senator William B. Allison and General Alfred A. Terry was sent to the Sioux to negotiate for the sale of Pa Sapa, the sacred Black Hills. Spotted Tail went to the Hills to see for himself just what it was the white men wanted. He found another expedition there, escorted by soldiers under Colonel Richard I. Dodge. The government was making sure about the reported gold, and had sent a professor, Walter P. Jenney, to see for them.

The Commission met September 17, 1875. The Indians were in no mood to sell Pa Sapa. That was sacred medicine ground. If it went to the white man, that was just another feast of crackers and molasses for the chiefs, and the white man would have made a long step back to where he had been in 1868.

Over seven thousand Indians gathered at the council. Most of them were hostile, and constant threats were made toward the commissioners. Only a firm stand by the friendly Indians under Young-Man-Afraid-of-His-Horses averted a massacre.

There was much talk. Spotted Tail knew that his people had a hill of gold; he wanted full value for it. Fast Bear said, "Our Great Father has a big safe, and so have we. This hill is our safe. We want seventy million dollars for the Black Hills." Red Cloud demanded Texas steers for meat and for seven genera-

In Castle Creek Valley—"The Thieves' Road."
Custer's long wagon train wound its way
through the Pa Sapa, the sacred hills.

California Joe. An expedition guided by California Joe, famous western scout, was sent to check Custer's report. Professor Walter Jenney, a geologist, head of the expedition, agreed that the Black Hills were a mountain of gold.

tions to come, and much money besides. Little Big Man screamed for war. Crazy Horse, who did not attend the council, observed that "One does not sell the earth upon which the people walk."

The council broke up without any agreement, and the commissioners went home with their bellies full of threats. They did not feel safe until they had crossed the Missouri. Fortune hunters moved into the Black Hills in increasing numbers. When the Indians found them, they killed them. But within six months, there were eleven thousand whites in Custer City alone.

In December, 1875, the Interior Department sent word to all the Indians in unceded territory, mostly on the Powder River, to come in to the reservation by January 31, 1876, or be considered "hostile." This was one way of clearing the Thieves' Road since the Commission had failed. But it was the middle of a severe winter. Even the white soldiers had stopped campaigning in November because of the cold. The Indians could have left their camps and come down to the agency, but they could see no reason for hurry. It was foolish to leave buffalo country for the agency where everyone knew food was scarce. "We will come when the snow melts," they said.

February 1, 1876, came, and the Interior Department notified the War Department that the Indians who had not come in were to be forced. That was the job of the army, and the army had its soldiers waiting. Already in March, 1875, General Crook, who had brought the Apaches on reservations, had been transferred to the Department of the Platte. He was going to teach these northern Indians to walk the white man's road. He was going to "use a little force." But a little was not going to be enough.

II

It was March, the Moon of Snowblindness, 1876. After a short February thaw, the snow was again deep on the ground, and ice frozen thick on the rivers. Sheltered in a canyon near the mouth of the Little Powder were the lodges of He Dog, Oglala Sioux, and Two Moons, Cheyenne; one hundred and five lodges altogether.

He Dog was waiting for the snow to melt before he came in to the agency. Only the month before he had

Little Big Man.   A commission was sent to get the Black Hills from the Sioux peacefully, but the warriors opposed any treaty. Little Big Man wanted war. He was in favor of beginning by exterminating the commission.

parted with Crazy Horse, who would not come in. There were stories of many white men coming north, soldiers, but the camp felt safe in the protecting canyon.

At dawn on March 17, a young Sioux left his tent to drive the horse herd to water. He went down a small ravine outside of camp, and was suddenly confronted by a line of cavalry trotting toward the village. With a yell he warned the sleeping lodges. A squaw lifted the flap of her tipi and saw the charge rising from the ravine. "The soldiers are here!"

He Dog, Two Moons, and the other warriors roused themselves quickly, and cut their way out of their lodges, bows, arrows, and guns in hand. The pony soldiers galloped into the village, shooting their revolvers. The warriors shot back, aiming at the horses, for a cavalryman on foot was but half a man.

The squaws and children, half clad, fled into the plum thicket around the camp, and clambered up the icy buffs behind the village. More soldiers followed the first, and drove the horse herd away from camp, almost seven hundred ponies in all.

The soldiers had taken the camp, but Indian warriors were on three sides, shooting, and keeping them from moving on. Suddenly smoke billowed from the lodges. Everything was being piled together and burned, all the buffalo meat and robes, the weapons and sacred medicine things. Nothing was to be left.

But the soldiers behaved strangely under fire. They turned around and left camp as quickly as they had come. The fight was not going the way they had planned. One of the soldier detachments never reached the village, and those who had could not face the shooting of the warriors. In their hurry, they even left their dead behind.

When the soldiers were gone, the Indians came back to their village. A few, poor horses which had been missed were gathered. Two Moons and He Dog went back to the village of Crazy Horse. Some of the warriors stayed behind to recapture a few ponies. They

Young-Man-Afraid-of-His-Horses. Only the intervention of Young-Man-Afraid-of-His-Horses and other friendly Indians saved the lives of the commissioners.

Spotted Tail and Fast Bear. Fast Bear (*right*), in his speech to the commissioners, referred to Custer's trail as "the Thieves' Road." Spotted Tail spoke for peace, but demanded full value for the hills.

General George Crook. Failing to get the
Black Hills peaceably, the whites decided to
use force. General Crook, who had gathered
in the Apaches, was sent up to deal with the
Sioux and Cheyennes. He ordered them to
gather on the reservations. Not all obeyed.

Two Moons. In March 1876 a band of
Cheyennes under Two Moons and Sioux
under He Dog were camped near the mouth
of the Powder River. A detachment of soldiers
under Colonel J. J. Reynolds attacked the
camp without warning. The Indians were
driven from their tipis into the snow. The
warriors rallied and drove the soldiers away,
but not before the camp was burned and all
the winter robes and meat destroyed.

succeeded in getting back over half the herd, but while driving them along, they ran into another detachment of soldiers, who took the horses away again.

The cavalry attack on the Sioux-Cheyenne village was the only major fight of General Crook's campaign in the winter of 1875–76. The campaign had started from Fort Fetterman on March 1 with ten cavalry and two infantry companies, with pack train and wagons. The detachment in the attack was led by Colonel J. J. Reynolds, Third Cavalry, guided by Sioux scouts.

Reynolds' fight on the Powder made it plain to the Indians that they would again have to unite to make a determined stand against the white man. It would be harder this time, because the white soldiers were being helped by agency Indians and traders' sons. Even those who had once shared the lodges of the Sioux were now leading the soldiers against them. Frank Grouard, who had once been welcome in the lodge of Crazy Horse, led Reynolds to the camp on the Powder. The warriors saw him there.

Deadwood, South Dakota, 1876. Only seven years after the white men had left their forts in the Sioux country and promised peace, they were already coming back. The lure of gold was stronger than the words of the 1868 treaty, and soon the frontier towns bordering the Black Hills swarmed with prospectors. With them came soldiers.

6

THE VISION OF SITTING BULL

I

SEVEN WINTERS HAD PASSED since the white man promised peace with the Sioux "so long as the grass shall grow." The abandoned forts were beaten by the rains of seven springs, and their charred ruins were fast returning to the soil from which they had sprung.

But now the white man was coming back. The treaty words were lost in the roaring of the new word—*Gold!* The fights would have to be made all over again.

In April, 1876, Sitting Bull, Hunkpapa Sioux, held a great council at Chalk Buttes on the Tongue River. Crazy Horse, with Two Moons and He Dog, suffering from Reynolds' attack on their camp on the Powder, went to the council. It was the time of the new grass, and the restless Indians from the reservations began, once more, to leave for the buffalo country. They came to the camp of Sitting Bull. Northern Cheyennes and Arapahoes, too, joined the big encampment. Seven great circles of lodges spread over the valley of the Tongue.

The talk was all for war. Three Stars, General Crook, had been at Red Cloud agency to recruit young warriors as scouts in the coming campaign. Red Cloud, Red Dog and Red Leaf stopped those who would have gone with the white soldiers to fight their

Sitting Bull. With the arrival of prospectors, the Sioux warrior and medicine man knew that the time had come to fight again. In April 1876 he held a great council. Sioux, Cheyennes, and Arapahoes gathered to decide what should be done.

own people, and Three Stars went away, angry. Surely it was a time to fight together, not brother against brother! "The whites want war," Sitting Bull observed, "and we will give it to them."

First, however, there was meat to get. Scouts reported buffalo in the Rosebud country, and the great camp moved to where the hunting was good. As they moved, the Indians were joined by new bands coming in from the agencies and elsewhere. Black Elk and his band came in from the shelter of the reservation, knowing well that war was near. Even the old Santee warrior, Inkpaduta, with a few lodges, joined them. Never before had the warriors gathered in such numbers—Crazy Horse, Big Road, Sitting Bull, Gall, Black Moon, Crow King, Spotted Eagle, Fast Bull, Touch the Clouds, Two Moons, Old Bear—all great warriors, chiefs or medicine men.

It was well that the warriors were many and the chiefs great. On May 17, General Alfred H. Terry, with six hundred men and horses, and four hundred infantry, started from Fort Abraham Lincoln. General John Gibbon had already left Fort Ellis, Montana, with four hundred fifty infantry. He had seen that there were many Indians near the mouth of the Rosebud.

General Crook, too, with over a thousand soldiers left Fort Fetterman on May 29, and moved toward Tongue River. The white soldiers were coming from every direction. General Terry hunted for Sitting Bull on the Little Missouri, and ordered Gibbon to help him. The Indians had not yet been found.

During the second week in June, the great Sioux-Cheyenne camp moved from the mouth of the Rosebud to the head of Ash Creek. Here was held the great yearly Sun Dance, sacred ceremony of the summer solstice.

Sitting Bull was one of those who sought a vision in the Sun Dance. A hundred small pieces of flesh were cut from his arms with an awl and sharp knife. Bleeding from his wounds, the chief gazed at the sun from

Record of a Mission. At the Red Cloud agency, General Crook, known to the Indians as Three Stars, was trying to recruit young warriors for the battle that was coming. Crook's visit to the agency in 1876 was recorded as shown above in the Sioux calendar.

dawn to dusk, seeking power, a vision to help his people. Finally he fell, exhausted and unconscious. When he rose again, he spoke to the people. Sitting Bull had seen a vision of many soldiers coming into camp upside down. The people were satisfied. Victory was certain.

A test of Sitting Bull's vision came soon. On June 16, five Cheyenne warriors out on a hunt and horse-stealing expedition spied a column of soldiers in the valley of the Rosebud. They rode back to camp quickly, sounding the wolf-howl of danger. Three Stars was only a day's march away! He had Crow and Shoshone scouts with him!

The warriors were hot for a fight, the vision strengthening them. Eagerly they rallied about the chiefs, and it was decided to attack Three Stars where he was, rather than wait for the soldiers to attack the camp. Over a thousand warriors gathered and set out for the valley of the Rosebud. Among them was Sitting Bull, still weak from the Sun Dance. With them, too, was Buffalo Calf Road Woman, sister of Chief Comes-In-Sight. With such warriors defeat was impossible.

Crook's column of cavalry and mule-mounted infantry had come to a halt along the Rosebud at the mouth of a canyon. The great Sioux village was supposed to be just a little farther down. Soon the "renegades" and "hostiles" would learn how foolish they had been to resist the wishes of the Great Father.

Rifle shots from scouts in the advance were the first warning of attack. Then came the great war cry, "Lakota, Lakota! Sioux, Sioux!" The warriors, in full fighting array appeared suddenly in front of the cavalry on the right flank of the column.

Mounted on their small, wiry ponies, a strong rawhide rope drawn tightly just back of the forequarters to serve as saddle, the Indians bent low, shooting from under the necks of their mounts. When a soldier fell, the nearest Indians dashed to his body and struck him with their *coup* sticks—the real glory moment of any fight or hunt.

The Indian attack seemed to be unplanned, but their method of fighting was different. The red warriors had learned something from the white soldiers. They learned the power of a cavalry charge, and the importance of keeping the detachments of soldiers apart. To that end, small bodies of Indians attacked the separated groups of soldiers again and again, preventing them from forming a skirmish line, a single, strong front.

Crook sent nine companies of soldiers under Anson Mills toward the narrow canyon, where he believed the Indian village was hidden. But the warriors attacked the remaining force so fiercely that the detachment was recalled.

All day the fight raged. Many brave deeds were done on both sides. The warriors counted fewer *coups,* but their war-making was better. By evening, fifty-seven of the soldiers had been killed or wounded, and only eighteen warriors were hurt. It was not a big fight if you counted the number of scalps, but it was enough to show Three Stars that the Indians were strong, and had learned something about fighting. Crook moved back to his wagon train on the Tongue and licked his wounds. He would hunt the Sioux no longer until he had more men.

Crook's Camp at Fort Fetterman. Crook set out from his camp with more than a thousand troops and plenty of ammunition. He was looking for Sioux.

The warriors returned in triumph to the big camp on Ash Creek. A four-day scalp dance followed. The keening of the women for the lost ones was not heard for the loudness of the victory songs. The medicine of Sitting Bull was strong.

II

While the Sioux-Cheyenne camp was dancing the scalp dance, more soldiers were gathering for another fight. Terry and Gibbon had given up hunting for Sitting Bull on the Little Missouri, and had reached the mouth of the Rosebud on June 21. Here they were met by Major Marcus A. Reno, with most of the Seventh Cavalry which had been sent on a reconnaissance up the Powder River to the Rosebud, almost to where Three Stars lost his fight. Here they had seen a great Indian trail leading across the divide toward the Little Big Horn River. The Indians had been located. Now it was time to make plans.

General Terry divided his forces. The Seventh Cavalry under Colonel Custer was to march up the Rosebud, find the Indian trail, and follow it, while Terry would march Gibbon's infantry up the Big Horn, reaching the Little Big Horn and rejoining Custer on June 26.

The white soldiers moved off on their planned march. The great Indian camp again moved down Ash Creek, this time to the valley of the Little Big Horn. It was a grand sight. Five great circles of lodges were strung along the west side of the river for three miles. Sitting Bull and his Hunkpapas were farthest up, a little above the mouth of Ash Creek. Then came the Miniconjous, the Oglalas, and the Sans Arcs. Farthest down of all was the mighty circle of Cheyenne lodges.

The Indians knew that the soldiers were coming. Box Elder, Cheyenne prophet, proclaimed that they were near at hand. But no one was afraid. The warriors were strong.

Sioux Sun Dance. At the great annual Sun Dance during the second week in June, Sitting Bull danced all day, looking for power, seeking a vision. Finally it came: many soldiers falling into camp.

Long Hair and Friends. Custer, now a lieutenant colonel, left from Fort Abraham Lincoln (near which this picture was taken) to fight the Sioux. He is standing in the center, arms folded. To his immediate right, seated, is his wife. Seven of the men in this group were to die on the Little Big Horn.

Chief Gall. After the Rosebud battle, the Sioux moved into a new camp on the Little Big Horn river. Here, on the morning of June 25, the Seventh Cavalry attacked the Indians. Gall, warrior of the Hunkpapa Sioux, met Major Reno's detachment, driving them across the river to the bluffs. "It was like chasing buffalo," said Gall and his warriors, "a great chase."

Low Dog. Low Dog, fighting Sioux chief, counted many *coups* in the fight at the Little Big Horn.

On the evening of June 24, Sitting Bull again offered up a prayer for strength and victory. That same evening, Colonel Custer prayed for victory for his own peculiar reasons. He told his Ree scouts that he alone was going to destroy the Sioux nation in one great blow, and that partly as a reward for his victory, he would some day become the Great Father in Washington. The scouts were doubtful about both promises.

On the morning of June 25, the Indians proceeded about their work, as usual. Crazy Horse went down to visit in the Cheyenne camp. Suddenly a great dust was seen in the valley above the Hunkpapa camp. The soldiers had come! They were coming into the camp as Sitting Bull had promised!

The warriors rushed from the lower camps, making ready for the fight. There were only a few soldiers coming toward them, a little over a hundred. It was easy. Easier than on the Rosebud. These troops, under Major Reno, had crossed the river about four miles above the camp, and moved toward it at a trot. But they never reached it.

Fierce gunfire from a thousand Indian guns wilted the little detachment. In a few minutes, twenty-nine soldiers were dead, and many wounded. Those who were able fled across the river to the safety of bluffs and woods, closely followed by the triumphant warriors after, "a great chase."

The pursuit was interrupted by an alarm from the other end of the camp. Soldiers were attacking here, too. The soldier chief on the bluff was left with a few warriors watching him, while the rest of the Indians streamed through the camp to the place of new danger across from the ford by the Miniconjou camp.

Here the soldiers had come down a ravine and threatened to charge across into the camp. But a great deed was done: four Cheyenne warriors held the soldiers for a few minutes, and waded across the river through the bullet hail. It was enough time for more warriors to come up and drive the soldiers away.

The column turned, and began to move down the

Custer's Last Rally. The Sioux and
Cheyennes crossed the river and attacked the
Seventh Cavalry soldiers from both ends.
Not a soldier was left alive. Sitting Bull's
vision had been strong.

east side of the river toward the lower end of the Indian camp, where there was another ford. Some of the
soldiers were on a ridge overlooking the river, and
others were between the ridges and the river.

Truly the eyes of the white soldier chiefs were
blinded that day! The Cheyenne and Sioux warriors
crossed the Little Big Horn at the Miniconjou ford,
and also at the lower end, by the Cheyenne lodges.
The column of soldiers was struck, front and rear.
Every rock, bush and ravine was friendly to the Indians. The soldiers were attacked on every side. When
those on the ridge were silenced, the warriors charged
up the ridge with a loud shout. Hoka Hey! The soldiers between the ridge and the river backed from the
charge.

"After that the fight did not last long enough to light
a pipe."

Crow King. This Sioux warrior fought hard at the Little Big Horn for his land, his freedom, and his people. Later years found him a scout, a pay-soldier for the white man.

White-Man-Runs-Him. A Crow scout employed by Custer, White-Man-Runs-Him led Lt. James Bradley of Terry's command to the battlefield where Custer and his men lay dead. The Sioux and Cheyennes had gone from the valley, leaving a trail toward the Big Horn mountains.

It was hard to believe. Never had such a victory been won, so many *coups* counted, so much plunder taken. A few Cheyennes from the south country found that the soldier coats taken from the dead were the same as those seen at the battle on the Washita years before, and their hearts were glad. But the soldier chief, Long Hair, Custer, was not found. Later it was learned that he was among the dead, but his hair was cut short, and he looked like any other man.

The soldiers on the bluff across from the opposite end of camp tried to move away while the fight was raging away from them, but the warriors returned quickly, and drove them back into their holes. All night the warriors besieged the soldiers, and the next morning tried to drive them out to where they could be killed. But the hill was a good place to fight. These few soldiers were not worth the trouble of a big charge, and so the Indians left them. The victory could not be made greater.

Besides, more soldiers were coming up the Big Horn. The Indians went back to their village about noon on June 26, and began to strike their lodges. The grass in the valley was fired, and behind the screen of smoke, the Sioux and Cheyennes slowly moved away toward the Big Horn mountains. The battle of the Little Big Horn was over. Two hundred sixty-six soldiers had been killed or mortally wounded. Fifty-four were wounded and recovered.

Indeed, many soldiers had fallen into camp upside down.

After the great victory on the Little Big Horn, the Sioux and Cheyennes went to the Big Horn mountains to cut lodge poles. The council fires were filled with much talk about the big fights. There was much dancing and feasting that summer. The white soldier chiefs had come, and had been defeated. No others had come to take their places. It was a good time. Perhaps the treaty would be kept, now, and the Black Hills saved. So, at least, thought the hopeful ones.

In the fall the Indians began their eastward move-

Curley. News of the Indian victory at the Little Big Horn was brought by Curley, a Crow scout, who saw what was happening and escaped before the end of the fight. He reached the steamer *Far West* at the mouth of the Little Horn, and by signs told the unbelieving soldiers of the disaster that had struck the Seventh Cavalry.

Rain-in-the-Face. Rain-in-the-Face had long hated the soldiers. He had been present when Fetterman and his troops had been wiped out. He had suffered in prison, arrested by Tom Custer, and is said to have promised to "cut the heart out of Tom Custer and eat it." A wound received at the Little Big Horn lamed him for life but did not dim his victory song. He lived to sing it a long time.

112

ment, as usual, toward the agencies, to hole up for the winter. But news from the reservations was not good. Indians who went in had their guns and horses taken from them. The friendly Indians were again urged to give up the sacred Hills. The whites prayed over the reservation Indians, and then threatened to starve them if they did not agree.

Many of the warriors did not go back. Many of them joined Crazy Horse on the Powder, wintering with the buffalo. Others attached themselves to Sitting Bull, north of the Yellowstone.

Grave of the Seventh Cavalry. The dead were buried and identified when possible. The battlefield of the Little Big Horn is still a cemetery.

Lodges at Peace. After defeating Custer at the Little Big Horn, the Indians spent the month of July, 1876, in small camps along the base of the Big Horn mountains, hunting, cutting lodge poles, and feasting. After this the warriors of Sitting Bull and Crazy Horse separated.

7

THE WARRIORS
COME IN

I

DURING THE AFTERNOON of Sunday, June 25, 1876,
Captain Anson Mills, Third Cavalry, restless from
long waiting, made a scout from the camp of General
George Crook on Goose Creek, Wyoming Territory.
Far to the northwest the Captain saw a great column
of smoke or dust in the air. He called the attention of
his fellow-officers to the column, and they agreed that
either some Indians were setting fire to the grass, or
perhaps there was a forest fire in the mountains.

Their guess was correct. There was smoke in the
air. It was the smoke of battle rising above the death of
the Seventh Cavalry on the Little Big Horn.

General Crook's command remained in the general
area of Goose Creek after the defeat on the Rosebud.
No move was made toward a junction with Terry who
was supposed to be moving south from the Yellowstone. There had been no news from Terry for a long
time, and no one knew how the other commands of the
Yellowstone expedition were faring. Crook had suffered much on the Rosebud, and was in no mood to
make a march until orders and reinforcements arrived.

Rumor, the harbinger of truth, began to circulate in
Crook's camp. Among the Shoshone and Ute allies it
was said that many pony soldiers had been killed in a
big fight to the north. Truth, however, did not arrive

115

until July 10, twenty days after Custer fell. On that day Ben Arnold and Louis Richaud came into camp with news of the massacre. For once rumor had been less than truth. Here was another, greater disaster to add to the toll of the Rosebud fight. The Sioux and Cheyennes were really making war this summer.

Three Stars was building up his strength to fight the Indians on at least equal terms. On August 3, the command was joined by Colonel Wesley Merritt with ten companies of the Fifth Cavalry and seventy-six recruits. The command now numbered over two thousand men. Merritt brought with him "Buffalo Bill" Cody, who had hurried from "theatrical engagements" in the east to participate in the late phases of the campaign. Only a few days before, Cody had added a famous chapter to his exploits by his supposed hand-to-hand encounter with chief Yellow Hand of the Cheyennes at the fight on War Bonnet Creek.

Crook was now ready to move. He separated his command from its wagon train, and arranged to operate with mule train alone, discarding all but the most essential equipment, rations, and ammunition. Traveling light, he believed, was the only way to catch Indians if they fled. Crook hoped that the Sioux, emboldened by two victories, would make a third attempt. If they did, they would fail.

The warriors of Sitting Bull, Crazy Horse and their Cheyenne allies had no intention of making another big fight. Enough for one season had been accomplished in June. July was spent hunting and feasting along the base of the Big Horns, and then the Indian bands separated. Sitting Bull went beyond the Yellowstone, and Crazy Horse to the Bear Butte country on the Little Missouri.

When on August 11 Crook and Terry finally met, thirty miles below the Yellowstone, they found no Indians between them. The combined commands returned to the river, and then parted, Terry going north on the trail of Sitting Bull, and Crook southeast toward the Black Hills on the trail of the other Indian bands.

Colonel Wesley Merritt. Until Merritt, with
detachments of the Fifth Cavalry, arrived at
Goose Creek, Wyoming Territory, on August
3, 1876, General Crook felt his forces were
too weak to encounter the Indians. News of
the Custer massacre had reached Crook on
July 10, increasing his respect for the
strength of the Sioux warriors.

Captain Jack Crawford. Crawford, a poet-
scout, was one of the guides Colonel Merritt
brought with him. Captain Jack was a gaudy
individual who wrote and published some
prairie grass-roots poetry. The books did not
sell very rapidly, so the author autographed
almost every copy, adding an extra, on-the-
spot verse gratis. He was more successful
as a scout.

The Utes and Shoshones, who had served as scouts for the Yellowstone expedition, went back to their tribes disgusted with such poor war-making. Buffalo Bill went east to his clamoring audiences.

Of those who were left with Three Stars, only Frank Grouard knew something of the country, and could guide the command to the Black Hills. The way was rough, there was almost constant rain, and no firewood. There were no Indians to fight, either. The mud was deep, and the expedition slogged its heavy way toward the end of a fruitless campaign.

Besides the ordinary hardships of the march, the command began to suffer from short rations. Three Stars had not counted on such a long march. He had hoped to find an Indian village full of dried meat to subsist the soldiers. But all the Indians were in front, and they kept their villages out of the way.

Slowly and painfully, the cavalry and infantry plodded along. Food became so scarce that horses had to be killed and eaten. "If we march long enough we will eat up the cavalry," was the grim joke of the foot soldiers. Some of the men broke down, weeping with exhaustion.

On September 8, General Crook sent Captain Mills ahead of the command with one hundred fifty men and the best horses. They were to bring supplies from the Black Hills settlements. Tom Moore, chief packer, went along with the strongest pack mules. Frank Grouard went as guide.

During the day, Grouard saw some Indian hunters in the distance, and found fresh pony tracks along a stream near Slim Buttes. He knew that there was an Indian camp nearby. It would be full of meat from the summer hunts, and there would be buffalo robes for the cold, wet soldiers. The Captain decided to attack the village.

Early on the morning of September 9, after the Indian village had been located, Captain Mills divided his detachment into three groups. The first, twenty-five mounted men under Lt. Frederick Schwatka, was

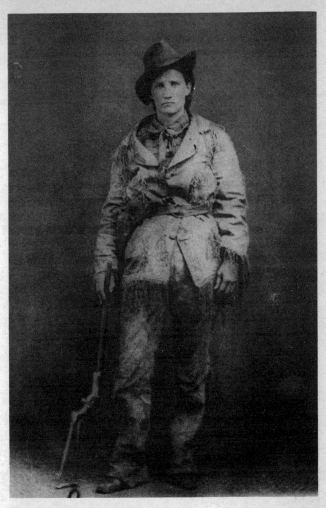

Calamity Jane. With the arrival of
reinforcements, Crook set out once again to
hunt the 'ndians, using pack mules as
transport. The packers and muleskinners were
a rough lot. Among them, it was said, was
Jane Canary, better known as Calamity Jane.

Commissary. Crook's forces on the Yellowstone expedition found their march difficult; rain, mud, and unfamiliar country delayed the column. Rations ran short, and the cavalry began to shoot horses for food.

American Horse (Iron Plume). The camp of American Horse, Sioux chief, at Slim Buttes was in the path of Crook's hungry soldiers. An advance party under Captain Mills, on its way to Deadwood for rations, attacked the camp, killing the chief, and seizing the winter supply of dried buffalo meat.

to charge the camp and stampede the horses. The other two groups, under Lts. Emmet Crawford and A. H. Von Leuttwitz, were to dismount and attack the village from right and left.

It was a cold, wet morning, and the strings of the lodges were slippery and stiff. When stampeding horses and rifle shots wakened the Sioux camp the warriors opened their lodges with knives, picked up their weapons and ran across the river, leaving their camp to the soldiers. From across the river, and from the bluffs on three sides, the warriors fought back at the invaders. Captain Mills sent back messengers to Crook, asking for help.

When the main body of troops arrived about noon, the village with its forty lodges was still held by soldiers. The hungry ones ran about wildly, filling their bellies with dried meat. The Sioux, led by chief Iron Plume, known to the whites as American Horse, had taken refuge in a small ravine beyond the river, and some soldiers were trying to force them out. The Indians had sent runners to the camp of Crazy Horse, nearby, and were expecting help.

Baptiste Pourier, "Big Bat," guide and interpreter, who knew the Indians well, spoke to them during a lull in the fight, asking them to surrender. Eleven squaws and six papooses were delivered from the pit of death, and then the fight raged on. Once more Big Bat spoke to the warriors, promising that no harm would come to them.

This time the old chief and his warriors gave up. Iron Plume had been shot in the belly. With his hands, he pressed in his intestines. He bit on a piece of wood to help bear the pain of his wound. Doctor V. T. McGillycuddy examined the chief and told him he would die. The old warrior held himself proudly to the end, passing without a complaint.

When the plundering of the lodges was at its height, the promised help from Crazy Horse and about six hundred of his warriors arrived. They appeared on the bluffs around the camp, and began pouring carbine fire

Lodge at Slim Buttes, with Seventh Cavalry Guidon. The Sioux village of American Horse was held by Mills's advance guard until the main body of troops arrived. After that, not even Sioux reinforcements under Crazy Horse were able to save the lodges. Among the camp plunder was booty from the battle of the Little Big Horn.

on the command. The plundering stopped, and a new fight raged. The soldiers formed a great ring around the village, and moved in rushes toward the bluffs. Even up the bluffs they went, their rifles driving the Sioux out of range. The warriors, outnumbered and outshot, their war spirit no longer burning as it had three months before, drew away. The soldiers of the Yellowstone expedition had one victory, small though it was.

The fight cost the Indians ten killed, while three soldiers had died, and twenty were wounded. The victory added these last men to the terrible price paid for the expedition of 1876.

General Crook and the horse-meat marchers reached the Belle Fourche on September 12, where rations from Deadwood met the command. After a few days at Deadwood, the General went to Fort Laramie for a conference with Sheridan. The rest of the command stayed in the Hills, recuperating from a fruitless campaign.

II

Bloodshed and scalp dances on the Little Big Horn did not lessen the greed of the white men for the Black Hills. The stream of fortune hunters flowed ever wider, and the heart of the Sacred Hills was burrowed into as if by so many prairie dogs. The claims of the Indians were brushed away with one hand while the other dipped the gold pan.

The white chiefs in Washington, too, decided that the Hills must be had at any price. In August, 1876, another commission was sent to the Sioux. George W. Manypenny, Bishop H. B. Whipple, and A. S. Gaylord were among those charged with the task of stealing the Black Hills. These treaty makers did not ask the Indians what they wanted, they told them what they would get. Bishop Whipple prayed to the Great Spirit to give wisdom to the Indian chiefs, and asked

Charging Bear. Charging Bear, one of American Horse's warriors, went with Crook as a captive and soon after enlisted as a scout.

Rest Camp. The "horse-meat marchers" plodded on after the battle of Slim Buttes, reaching the Belle Fourche river on September 12. Here, supplied with rations from Deadwood, the Yellowstone expedition rested, each man celebrating the fact that he was yet alive.

125

that the commission might "help the poor and perish-ing."

Judge Gaylord spoke another language. He informed the Sioux that they would either sign or starve, for the treaty was part of the law appropriating money for Indian rations.

Red Cloud, Spotted Tail, and the other reservation Indians knew the truth of the harsh words, but they raised their voices in final protest. The fight at the Little Big Horn had not been their doing. "Rub it out," said Red Cloud. "Tell the people that this is not an Indian war; it is a white man's war. A great many widows and orphans have been made on both sides. It is displeasing to the Great Spirit."

The cheeks of the commissioners were red with shame, but they had been sent to get the Hills, and could do nothing else.

Not only were the Sioux to give up their sacred Hills, but they were to move again; this time to Indian Territory, if they chose, or to the old place on the Missouri. Neither place was welcome to the Indians. It was a case of move or starve, explained Judge Gaylord. The Indians had better sign.

Standing Elk had heard enough. He had kept a count, and this was the tenth time he had been asked to sign the treaty papers of the white man. "My friend," he told the Judge, "your speech is as if a man had knocked me on the head with a stick. By your speech you have put great fear upon us. Whatever the white people say to us, wherever I go, we all say yes to them—yes, yes, yes. Whenever we don't agree to anything that is said in council they give us the same reply, 'You won't get any food! You won't get any food!' "

But the Indians signed. Red Cloud, Fast Bear, and Red Leaf of the Oglalas, Spotted Tail and Standing Elk of the Brulés, John Grass of the Blackfeet, Standing Bear of the Miniconjous, White Ghost of the Yanctons, and a few others.

It was true that the treaty of 1868 had promised that no new treaty could be made without the agreement of and all the rights and privileges in Nebraska, and on the Republican Fork of the Smoky Hill River, secured to us by said treaty.

Provided – That we do not surrender any right of occupation of the country situated in Nebraska, North of the Divide, which is south of and near to the Niobrara River, and West of the 100th Meridian; but desire to retain that country for future occupation and use.

Little _{his} Wound, _{mark}	Taopi Chikisa	Chief
Pawnee _{his} Killer _{mark}	Stili kte	Sub-Chief
Black _{his} Bear _{mark}	Mato Sape	Sub-Chief
Iron _{his} Horse _{mark}	Ta xunkamaza	Soldier
Quick _{his} Bear _{mark}	Mato luza	Sub-Chief
Red _{his} Dog _{mark}	Xunkaluta	Chief
High _{his} Wolf _{mark}	Xunka manits wakanto	Chief
Conquering _{his} Bear _{mark}	Mato yui	Head Soldier
White Crane _{his} Walking _{mark}	Pahasa mani	Head Soldier
Tall _{his} Lance _{mark}	Wahukeza wakatu	Soldier
Bear's _{his} Robe _{mark}	Mato ha xina	Soldier
Red _{his} Leaf _{mark}	Warpexa	Chief
Day _{his} _{mark}	Ampa ha	Chief
Yellow _{his} Hair _{mark}	Pehizizi	Head Soldier
White _{his} Tail _{mark}	Sin te ska	Sub-Chief

Sign or Starve. In August 1876 a second commission was sent from Washington to the Sioux seeking to obtain the Black Hills. The commissioners presented a treaty, telling the Sioux, "Sign or starve." The warriors signed, as seen above on the first page of signatures of the original agreement.

Iron Nation. Iron Nation signed the agreement of 1876 for the Lower Brulé Sioux.

Little Wound. Little Wound, of the Bear People, an Oglala society, also signed.

John Grass. John Grass of the Blackfeet
also made his mark. His tribe had been a
symbol of terror to trespassing whites all
over the northwestern frontier. But he knew
that the old days were gone. He later signed
other papers and lost more land.

129

three-fourths of the adult males, but the officials said that this new treaty was only an "agreement." By this "agreement" the Indians lost the Black Hills, the unceded territory where the buffalo were, and were forced to choose a new home on the Missouri or in Indian Territory. The victories of the summor of 1876 counted as nothing.

Red Cloud sulked, and talked war. He would not stay at the agency, but moved about forty miles away on Chadron creek. He did not like the soldier chiefs who had taken over the agency in July. His friend, Red Leaf, moved with him. The soldiers, who were getting ready for another campaign, decided to bring in these two chiefs. On October 24, Pawnee scouts surrounded and captured the two camps, took all the arms and horses, and led the chiefs back to the agencies. General Crook, who was angry at Red Cloud's "obstinacy," deposed him, and declared Spotted Tail chief of all the reservation Sioux.

III

While the treaty makers were taking the Black Hills from the Sioux and Cheyennes, more soldiers were hurried from the east to fight the warriors who had killed so many soldiers during the summer. There were enough soldiers to replace all those killed on the Little Big Horn, and many, many more. The soldier chiefs believed now that it would take more than a "little force" to make the Indians walk the white man's road.

Among the soldiers sent to the fight was Bear Coat, Colonel Nelson A. Miles. In October, 1876, Miles went to the cantonment on the Tongue River, later known as Fort Keogh, and much equipment and supplies came with him.

Sitting Bull was in the country, too, and knew that either he or the soldiers would have to move. The chief asked Johnny Brughiere, half-breed interpreter

130

and adviser, to write a note to Miles. The note was posted on a cleft stick on the road to the fort:

> I want to know what you are
> doing on this road. You scare all
> the buffalo away. I want to hunt in
> this place. I want you to turn back
> from here. If you don't, I will
> fight you again. I want you to
> leave what you have got here, and
> turn back from here. I am your
> friend
>
>   Sitting Bull
> I mean all the rations you have
> got, and some powder. Wish you
> would write as soon as you can

But the Sun Dance vision that had fired the warriors in June had faded and grown cold. The soldiers laughed over the note, and kept on coming through the buffalo country.

On October 21, 1876, Sitting Bull had a council with Bear Coat north of the Yellowstone. The warriors had stolen a few mules, and attacked a supply train. Miles was after them. Sitting Bull knew of the betrayal of the reservation chiefs in August. He knew that the old days were gone, and that the land had been given away. But he asked for an old-fashioned peace, one which would let him trade for powder and ammunition, and allow him to stay in the north to hunt buffalo.

The council lasted two days, and ended in a fight. The soldiers were too strong. They had many guns, even quick-firing ones known as Gatlings. The warriors were driven back. Most of them finally asked for peace, but Sitting Bull, Gall, and one hundred nine lodges of Sioux moved up to the Grandmother Land, Canada, crossing the line in February, 1877.

The Sioux and Cheyennes who had gone to the Bear Butte country on the Little Missouri in the fall of 1876 were ready for a quiet winter. They had killed their

Sitting Bull's Council with General Miles. Sitting Bull and Bear Coat finally met in October 1876 north of the Yellowstone. The chief asked for an "old-fashioned peace," with a chance to trade for powder and bullets. He wanted to hunt buffalo for the winter. The council ended in a fight.

Red Shirt. Red Shirt was one of the many warriors who surrendered to Miles after the October 1876 fight.

High Bear. High Bear was not ready to walk the white man's road. With Sitting Bull, Gall, and other chiefs, one hundred nine lodges of Sioux moved to Canada in February, 1877.

buffalo, dried the meat, and repaired their lodges. It was not time to fight. Summer, when the days were long, and a warrior could fight without freezing to death—that was the time for war-making.

The whites felt otherwise. To them war-making was simply another way of getting pay. Winter was as good a time to fight as any. In fact it was a better time to fight Indians, because they would be separated into small camps, not all gathered together as they had been on the Little Big Horn.

With these things in mind, Three Stars, Crook, went out on another campaign known as the Big Horn expedition. With him were eleven companies of infantry, eleven of cavalry, and four of artillery. Many Indians joined as scouts; Pawnees, Sioux, Arapahoes, Shoshones, Bannocks, and a few Cheyennes. There were one hundred sixty-eight wagons, seven ambulances, and four hundred pack mules. The expedition, starting from Fort Fetterman on November 14, 1876, numbered over two thousand. Three Stars had learned something at the Rosebud.

The white soldiers were looking for the camp of Crazy Horse, supposed to be near the old Rosebud battleground. When the command reached the Crazy Woman fork of the Powder River, an agency Cheyenne came in and reported a large Cheyenne village, under Dull Knife, in the Big Horns near the head of Crazy Woman creek. Three Stars sent Colonel Ranald Mackenzie with the Indian scouts and all the cavalry to find and capture the village. The detachment started off November 24.

The Cheyennes, a camp of one hundred fifty lodges, knew that the soldiers were coming. Four scouts, Hail, Crow Necklace, Two Moons, and High Wolf had been spying on the troops. They reported many soldiers on the Powder, and Indian scouts with them speaking four languages. "If they reach this camp, I think there will be a fight," said Two Moons.

Some of the Cheyennes wanted to move, and join the Sioux camp not far away. But Last Bull, chief of the Fox Society, would not listen. "No one shall leave the camp. We will stay up all night and dance." It was the night of November 24, 1876.

Early the next morning, when the sky was getting a little light, and the dance was ended, the words of Two Moons came to pass. The white soldiers and Indian scouts swept into the valley from the north, charging through the camp, driving the Cheyennes from their lodges into the freezing dawn.

It was much like Reynolds' fight on the Powder, except that the soldiers fought better. The warriors retreated south and west, fighting at long range all day, slipping away during the night. They marched through the Big Horn mountains to the camp of Crazy Horse, where they found food and shelter.

The Cheyennes in Dull Knife's village had lost almost everything. Their lodges were in ashes, their horses taken, their meat and robes gone. Even their scared medicine things, and the trophies from the fight on the Little Big Horn were lost. Over forty warriors died in the defense of the camp. The white man wanted the land, and blood would not stop him.

IV

When the Cheyennes fled to the village of Crazy Horse after Mackenzie's raid, it was but another sign that the time of Indian resistance to the white man was coming to an end. No longer could the Sioux and Cheyennes set up their lodges in peace on the Powder or the Tongue. Most of the buffalo in the south land had already disappeared, and in the north they were fast becoming silent heaps for the bone wagons.

There was no new place to go. The Black Hills were taken away, the last hunting grounds were a pathway for the new iron road. The Grandmother Land, Canada, whither Sitting Bull had fled, was poor refuge. The soldiers in that country did not want raids across the border. They even scolded when the Indians went south after the few buffalo that were left.

Attack on the Sioux Camp. On January 8, 1877, General Miles's soldiers reached the main Sioux camp, and a battle followed. A blizzard blew up, and behind it the Sioux slowly moved away. All day the warriors held off the soldiers. Miles decided he had had enough winter fighting and went back to Fort Keogh. The following spring, however, Crazy Horse realized he could not win and surrendered.

Crazy Horse and his chiefs held council over these things. Their hearts were heavy. The war-spirit was low. Cartridges were hard to get, and the white soldiers were coming in ever greater numbers. Perhaps the time had come to get things by peace talk rather than war talk.

News from the agencies spoke for peace. Three Stars let it be said that if the warriors came in and made peace, they would be allowed to come back to the buffalo country to a reservation there. They would not have to go south to Indian Territory or to the place on the Missouri.

But the tongue of the white man had been crooked so often that the chiefs could not believe what was promised. Perhaps it would be better to go to the fort at the mouth of the Tongue and surrender to Bear Coat, who also spoke for peace.

136

Late in December, 1876, eight chiefs from the camp of Crazy Horse went to the fort to talk peace. When they neared the stockade, Crow scouts, pay soldiers for the whites, came out at them, shooting. Five of the peace talkers were killed. Crazy Horse had enough of that kind of peace talk, and moved his camp away.

Miles now dropped all pretense of peace, and went out with his soldiers after Crazy Horse and the Cheyennes. On January 1 and 3, the troops had little fights with the warriors of the rear guard, while the main Indian camp moved slowly up the Tongue. On the morning of January 8, the soldiers caught up with the main camp, and a big fight followed. A blizzard blew up, and hid the camp from view, and the Indians moved away once again. The warriors stayed, and held off the soldiers all day. Bear Coat had enough fighting for that winter, and moved back to the fort.

The winter passed, cold and dreary. Hunger and a heavy heart darkened the days. In February, Spotted Tail came out from the agency, talking peace to his people. He brought new promises from Three Stars about a place to live in the buffalo country. Crazy Horse listened to the promise. He knew that the time had come. The people would go in.

On the morning of May 6, 1877, Crazy Horse and his followers, eleven hundred in all, moved through the hills a few miles from Camp Robinson. This time the warriors came in peace. When Lt. W. P. Clark rode up to go with the chief into camp, Crazy Horse offered his left hand to the soldier, saying, "Friend, I shake with this hand because my heart is on this side; I want this peace to last forever." He Dog took his scalp shirt and put it on Clark to show that all war between them was done.

A little after noon, the procession of Indians wound out of the hills to the agency. First came Red Cloud at the head of the Indian soldier-guards. Then Crazy Horse, Little-Big-Man, Little Hawk, He Dog, Old Hawk, and Big Road. Behind the warriors, for two miles, moved the rest of the people with their ponies,

Crazy Horse. Crazy Horse was restless on the reservation. The soldiers, fearing that he would again go north with his warriors, attempted to put him in the guard house. Crazy Horse resisted and was stabbed to death. (Various photographs have been used to represent Crazy Horse, who boasted that his shadow would never be taken by the white man's magic box. A photograph of Race Horse has been published several times as that of Crazy Horse. S. J. Morrow labeled this photograph as Crazy Horse, and the curator of the Morrow collection at the University of South Dakota is inclined to believe this may be the Sioux chieftain.)

Camp at Pine Ridge, South Dakota. The death of Crazy Horse marked the end of all war-making by the Sioux. Red Cloud moved with his people to an agency at Pine Ridge. The old life was gone forever.

dogs, and lodges. Everyone was quiet until the warriors struck up the peace chant. The people joined in, holding their heads high, though their hearts were heavy. It was a victory march, not a surrender.

Then came the hard part—horses and guns were all taken away. Over two thousand four hundred ponies were taken that day, and one hundred seventeen guns. Little Hawk was wearing a silver medal given by the whites to his father at a peace conference on the Platte sixty years before. He was allowed to keep it.

Crazy Horse was restless on the "white man's island." The promise of a reservation in the buffalo country was never kept. The soldiers and Indian scouts watched every move the chief made, and reported it. Crazy Horse was a prisoner.

In September, the chief went up to the Spotted Tail agency. The whites were afraid that he was planning to go north with his people, so they arrested him, and tried to put him in the guard house at Camp Robinson. Crazy Horse resisted, and was stabbed to death in the fight. His arms were held by Little-Big-Man, one of his own chiefs.

The death of Crazy Horse marked the end of all war-making by the Sioux. From this time on, they walked the white man's road unless the white man himself pushed them off.

Red Cloud and Spotted Tail were finally forced to live on the Missouri, the old land where they did not want to be. After a short stay in this hated place, they again moved, in the spring of 1878. Red Cloud went to Pine Ridge, and Spotted Tail, with his people, to the Rosebud.

In July, 1881, Sitting Bull, whose followers had left him, came south and gave himself up at Fort Buford. He was sent to Standing Rock agency, where he lived on Grand River, near his birthplace.

When he surrendered, Sitting Bull knew the old life was gone forever. He sang a new song,

> A warrior
> I have been.
> Now
> It is all over,
> A hard time
> I have.

Dull Knife. After Mackenzie's raid on his camp near the head of Crazy Woman creek in November 1876, Dull Knife wintered with Crazy Horse. The northern Cheyenne chief surrendered in the spring of 1877 at Camp Robinson and his people moved to a reservation. Later he joined other Cheyennes in a decision to move north.

140

8

DULL KNIFE MARCHES HOME

THE FIGHTS OF the winter of 1876–77, followed by peace talk from the agencies, brought in both Sioux and Cheyennes. On April 22, 1877, a band of Cheyennes led by Two Moons, White Bull, Crazy Head, and other chiefs surrendered to Miles at Fort Keogh on the Tongue. The soldiers were glad to see them come in. There had been much fighting and killing. Peace was better. Thirty of the warriors enlisted as scouts under Miles.

Dull Knife and his people, who had wintered with Crazy Horse after Mackenzie's raid, surrendered in the spring of 1877 at Camp Robinson. General Crook held a council with the Cheyennes, telling them they could go either to Indian Territory, to the agency at Fort Washaskie, Wyoming, or stay at Camp Robinson for a year to decide.

It was plain, however, that Crook and the other soldiers wanted the Cheyennes to go south. The Indians decided to stay at Camp Robinson, but Standing Elk, who spoke for them in council, said they would follow the wishes of the white man and go to Indian Territory.

On May 1, 1877, nine hundred sixty northern Cheyennes, accompanied by a few soldiers, began the

141

long road south to Fort Reno, Indian Territory, the home of their relatives, the southern Cheyennes and the Arapahoes. Ninety days they traveled, moving through the land quietly, and reported to Fort Reno August 5.

The new home of the northern Cheyennes was different in every way from their old hunting grounds. Here the buffalo was almost gone, and other game was equally scarce. The Indians had to depend on tough Texas steers for meat. Sickness in the form of malarial diseases rode through the land. There were new, troublesome insects to bother them.

The southern Cheyennes did not welcome their relatives, calling them "fools," and "Sioux." As a result, the two tribes did not camp together. "They lived," said the agent at Fort Reno, "but that was about all."

Wild Hog reported, "Very soon after our arrival there the children began to get sick and to die. Between the fall of 1877 and the fall of 1878 we lost fifty children by sickness." The agency doctor did not have enough medicine for the sick Indians, and even if he had, there were five thousand Indians for one doctor.

But the greatest sickness of the Cheyennes was a longing for their old land. Little Chief, who had come from the north later, wanted to return, "Because that is the land where I was born, the land that God gave us; and because it was better than this in every way; everything is better up there than here, the soil is better, the water is better. I have been sick a great deal of the time since I have been down here—homesick and heartsick, and sick in every way. I have been thinking of my native country, and the good home I had up there, where I was never hungry, and when I wanted anything to eat could go out and hunt the buffalo. It does not make me feel good to hang about an agency and to have to ask a white man for something to eat when I get hungry."

About three hundred of the Cheyennes decided they would not stay at their new reservation any longer. In July, 1878, Little Wolf and some of his men went to

Near Fort Reno. The Cheyennes who surrendered were sent to Fort Reno, Indian Territory, in the south. The land was barren and windswept, hot and dusty. Tipis had to be protected by barricades of brush.

see agent John D. Miles. They told him they were going north. There was only one thing they asked. Little Wolf said that if the soldiers were sent after them, they should fight away from the agency. "I do not want the agency ground bloody," he explained.

The night of September 9, the Cheyennes took down their lodges and began their march north. There were eighty-nine men, one hundred twelve women, and one hundred thirty-four children. Their leaders were Dull Knife, Wild Hog, Little Wolf, and Tangle Hair. Little Wolf was head of the warriors, and the fugitives moved as he directed, for they knew that the soldiers would soon come after them.

Two days the Cheyennes moved north, to the Little Medicine Lodge River, where they camped. Here Indian police and white soldiers found them. There was a little talk about coming back, some threats, and then a fight. The shooting was started by the soldiers, for Little Wolf had told his warriors that the Cheyennes would only defend themselves, not attack. There were few bullets in the camp, and few guns. Besides, if they went north without attacking, they might be allowed to stay. Three soldiers were killed in this first fight, and five Cheyennes were wounded. The soldiers then went away; the Indians moved north once more.

There were several small fights during the next few days, but the soldiers were always too few, and Little Wolf always picked strong places to make a fight. Just south of the Arkansas River, the warriors found a party of buffalo hunters. From these hide hunters they took eighteen buffalo, many guns, and a good supply of ammunition.

The Indians crossed the Arkansas September 23, and moved north quickly. Five days later, on Punished Woman's Fork of the Smoky Hill River, many soldiers came up, and there was a big fight. Little Wolf had again found a good place. The leader of the soldiers, Colonel William H. Lewis, was killed, and several of his men wounded. Only one warrior was killed. The soldiers again went away.

Little Wolf. After about a year in the new country, some of the Cheyennes decided to go north, back to their old home. Little Wolf came to the agent and told him they were leaving. He asked only that the soldiers not try to stop them near the agency. "I do not want the agency ground bloody," he explained.

Cheyenne Camp Preparing to Move. On the night of September 9, 1878, the Cheyennes took down their lodges, loaded their travois, and struck north, toward home.

The Cheyennes did not stop for scalp dances, or to mourn their dead. They wanted to reach their old home as quickly as possible. Nothing was to stop them. Settlers who got in their way were killed. Fresh horses were stolen, and cattle was taken for meat. Some of the young warriors went wild and took many scalps. They could not help remembering that all this land had once been theirs, and the white man had taken it all away, giving nothing in return.

Across the Kansas Pacific Railroad the Cheyennes fled, over the South Platte River near Ogalala, over the Union Pacific line east of Sidney, Nebraska, and finally over the North Platte near the mouth of White Clay Creek. Troops were sent after them from every direction, from Laramie, Robinson, Sidney, Fort Dodge, and Fort Wallace, but the Indians succeeded in slipping past the marching columns. The Cheyennes were not looking for scalps, but for the good grass, good water, and the good hunting.

Beyond the North Platte, the fugitives separated. Little Wolf, with most of the warriors, went north toward the old land on the Powder. Dull Knife and one

Standing Them Off. As the Cheyennes moved north, they were pursued by soldiers and Indian police. However, they always managed to beat off or slip past their enemies.

Dull Knife's Defiance.   Dull Knife finally surrendered to the soldiers on October 23, 1878, and the Cheyenne captives were taken to Camp Robinson and housed in an unused barracks. In January 1879 they were told that they could not go home but would have to return south. Dull Knife spoke for his people: "I am here on my own ground, and I will never go back. You may kill me here, but you cannot make me go back."

hundred forty-eight followers went toward the place where the old Red Cloud agency had been.

On October 23, in the Sand Hills of Nebraska, Dull Knife and his people suddenly came face-to-face with two troops of the Third Cavalry under Captain J. B. Johnson. A heavy snow prevented both Indians and soldiers from finding each other sooner. The Cheyennes surrendered to Captain Johnson without a fight, asking to be taken to Camp Robinson or Sheridan.

For two days, the Captain councilled with the Indians to decide where they should go. By that time, more soldiers had come up, and Captain Johnson felt safe enough to tell the Indians that they would have to go to Camp Robinson.

Their guns were taken from them—at least all that the soldiers could find. Some guns were hidden away. The wife of Black Bear later explained, "I had a carbine hanging down my back." Other guns were taken apart, and the big parts hidden on the squaws, the small pieces worn as ornaments by the children.

The Cheyenne captives were housed in an unused barracks at Camp Robinson while the soldiers waited for official word as to what should be done with them. It was not a bad life at the camp. The Indians were allowed to wander away from the post during the day for a little hunting, but they had to come back at night to be counted. There were dances at the post, and the soldiers were very friendly.

There was much talk, however, about going south. The whites always told the Indians that they would probably be sent back to Indian Territory. The answer always came, "We will die first." But none of the soldiers really believed that.

On January 3, 1879, the Cheyennes were finally told that the White Father in the east had decided that they must return to Fort Reno. "It would upset the entire reservation system" if they were allowed to return to their old land.

Again the chiefs refused. "I am here on my own ground," Dull Knife said, "and I will never go back.

Left Hand. The Cheyenne captives were
denied food and water to "make them
agreeable" to returning south. In addition,
Left Hand and others were taken from the
barracks and put in irons by order of Captain
H. W. Wessells.

You may kill me here, but you cannot make me go back." Besides, it was the middle of winter, and the Indians were in rags.

The soldiers were no longer friendly. They threatened, and locked up the Indians in the old barracks. Still the Cheyennes would not submit. Their food was cut off; they would not change their minds. Water was kept from them; they would not go south. Four days they were without food, and two without water. They were ready to die.

The commanding officer, Captain H. W. Wessells, then took the warrior, Wild Hog, from the barracks and put him in irons. Old Crow, who had been a scout against the Sioux in 1876, came out with Wild Hog. They put him in irons, too.

The starving captives then decided that if they must die, it was better to die as warriors. The concealed guns were brought out and assembled. A pile of saddles and parfleches was set by a window, making it easy to climb out. The Cheyennes then said goodbye to each other, and were ready to go.

Shortly after dark on January 9, the Indians broke out of the barracks and ran toward the bluffs across White River, west of the post. They fled across the bridge near the sawmill. Five warriors stayed behind, keeping the soldiers busy until the others should have escaped.

There was much shooting on that cold, moonlight night. The five warriors who stayed behind were soon dead, and the soldiers started after the others who had escaped across the river. When daylight came, sixty-five captives, some wounded, had been brought back to the post. Fifty dead, frozen in the snow, were piled into wagons and brought in. Some of the wounded would not be taken. Big Antelope stabbed his wife and then killed himself.

The hunt then began for those who had escaped. They had fled eighteen miles northwest, and were found hidden on a knoll. These few Cheyennes drove the soldiers off, and fled farther. Once more they were

Prisoners. The imprisoned Cheyennes preferred to die fighting. On the night of January 9, 1879, Tangled Hair and Porcupine, with several other warriors, led the way out of the barracks. These leaders stayed behind, with guns they had concealed, and held off the soldiers until the other prisoners had escaped. Crow, Left Hand, and Wild Hog were in irons in the guardhouse and could not help. Both Tangled Hair and Porcupine were wounded and taken prisoner (*Lower row:* Wild Hog; George Reynolds, an interpreter; Old Man; Blacksmith. *Upper row:* Tangled Hair; Left Hand; Crow; Porcupine. Taken at Dodge City, Kansas, a few months later.)

discovered. Each time they were found, a soldier paid with his life for the finding.

Captain Wessells sent for help, and on January 18, he was joined by two companies of soldiers from Fort Laramie. Finally the troops surrounded the Indians in a hole on top of a bluff above Hat Creek. There were thirty-two Indians in the hole, and after the soldiers were done shooting, only three squaws were alive, and one of them was wounded. One of the dead squaws had stabbed her child and then herself.

After the prisoners had all been brought in, and the dead counted, it was found that eleven soldiers had been killed, and ten wounded. Of the Cheyennes, seventy-eight were captured and sixty-four were dead—they at least would never go south. Seven Indians were unaccounted for. "These last seven," said the report, "are women and children, and are supposed to have died on the bluffs."

General Crook, who had hoped for peace and wanted the Cheyennes to have a home in the north, wrote to the White Father in sorrow and anger. "Among these Cheyennes were some of the bravest and most efficient of the auxiliaries who had acted under General Mackenzie and myself in the campaign against the hostile Sioux in 1876 and 1877, and I still preserve a grateful remembrance of their distinguished services, which the government seems to have forgotten."

Dull Knife with his family escaped by hiding in a cave. He reached Pine Ridge agency after wandering in the cold for eighteen days. He lived there, and died about 1883.

The warriors under Little Wolf reached the hunting grounds on the Powder in March, but were met there by soldiers under White Hat, Lt. W. P. Clark, and surrendered to him. They were taken to Fort Keogh, and enlisted as scouts under Miles. A few years later, they were given a reservation on the Tongue.

They had come home.

Tongue River Reservation. The warriors
under Little Wolf surrendered near Fort
Keogh in March. They enlisted and served
faithfully as scouts under General Miles, and
were eventually given a reservation on the
Tongue River. Here, though they were not
free, they were on their home grounds.

Emigrant Train. Indians on the far Pacific coast had lived for many years under the Spanish rulers of California. But many members of the smaller northern tribes, such as the Modocs, had never seen white men until gold was discovered in 1848. When the Modocs saw their first emigrant wagon train passing through Lost River Valley, they were so startled that they ran in fright to the hills.

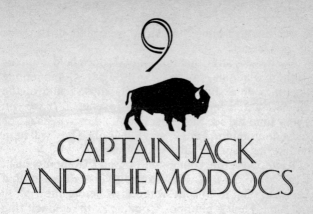

CAPTAIN JACK
AND THE MODOCS

LONG BEFORE the westward expansion of the United States, the Indians of the southern Pacific coast had been living under the Spanish rulers of California. In many sections, they had adopted the customs of the white men, and by the middle of the nineteenth century, conflict between the races was almost unknown.

When gold was discovered in 1848, however, new trails were opened into California and Oregon from the northern routes. Coastal Indians who had never seen white men now saw them for the first time. The Modocs, who lived along the shores of Tule Lake on the California-Oregon border, were so startled when they saw their first emigrant train that they ran for the hills. They thought the Great Spirit had sent evil messengers to punish them. Later when they lost their fear, the Modocs were friendly, but a series of unfortunate incidents soon turned this small and peaceful tribe into as fierce a band of killers as ever fought in the West.

After a party of Shastans had ambushed a wagon train near Alturas in 1853, the miners sent a posse scouring the countryside. These volunteers were out to kill every Indian they could find. Since the guilty Shastans were hiding, and the innocent Modocs were expecting no trouble, the latter were slain like rabbits in their camps.

For weeks after this raid, the Modocs held councils in the mountains, in the Lava Bed caves, and among the thick tules of the nearby marshes. Some of the chiefs wanted to fight a war of revenge. "If we run every time we see the white people, they will chase us from mountain to valley, and kill us all. They will hunt us like we hunt the deer and antelope."

Keintpoos, the young son of Chief Combutwaush, listened to this talk. He listened to his father say that he was going to kill the white men before they could kill him. Then Keintpoos stood up in the council ring and spoke: "I am a Modoc," he said. "I am not afraid to die, but that is not it. We have not killed any white people yet, so let us not kill any. No one told the white men who fire on us that it was the Shastans and not the Modocs who made the attack on their wagons. I see that the white people are many. We are few. If we value our lives or love our country, we must not fight the white men."

The words of Keintpoos were echoed by some of the Modoc leaders, but a few days later when an emigrant train came near the Lava Beds, the Indians attacked it. "The Massacre of Bloody Point," the white people called the affair, and a group of Oregon settlers led by Ben Wright volunteered to hunt down the guilty Indians. By pretending that they were still friends of the Modocs, the volunteers lured old Chief Combutwaush into a trap and killed him with many of his warriors. Keintpoos was now the leader of his father's people, and he convinced some of the Modocs that they must make a peace with the white men if they hoped to survive. A few recalcitrants, however, listened to a sub-chief, Schonchin, and his son, Schonchin John, who believed they should fight the invaders.

For two years, young Keintpoos sought the aid of friendly white settlers in Oregon and in northern California. Finally he received promises that the

Captain Jack. After a band of Shastan Indians ambushed a wagon train in 1853, many innocent Modocs were brutally killed by a posse of miners who recognized no differences between tribes. Some of the Modocs wanted to fight a war of revenge, but Keintpoos (Captain Jack) warned against it. "The white people are many," he said, "but we are few. If we value our lives or love our country, we must not fight the white men."

Modocs would not be harmed if they would remain in their Lost River country and not roam too widely afield. Elisha Steele, a lawyer of Yreka, California, proved to be their best friend. It was Steele who first gave Keintpoos the name of "Captain Jack," a name which was quickly adopted by both the white men and the Indians.

By the summer of 1864, however, the Lost River valley was becoming so thickly settled that the government issued an order to the Oregon Superintendent of Indian Affairs, instructing him to negotiate a treaty which would remove all the Indians in the Klamath and Modoc areas to a reservation. In the councils which followed, Captain Jack resisted all efforts of the commissioners to force the Modocs off their land. The clever government agents then refused to recognize Captain Jack as Modoc chief, and Old Schonchin was declared the legal head of the tribe. Schonchin of course signed the agreement immediately. To avoid violence, Captain Jack reluctantly added his signature.

From the beginning, the reservation plan was a failure, largely because the Modocs were forced to live with their traditional enemies, the Klamaths. As the reservation was on land which had always been Klamath territory, the Klamaths refused to allow the Modocs to cut timber or hunt game. Life soon became unbearable for the Lost River Indians. On a dark, moonless night in the spring of 1870, Captain Jack led about seventy of his braves and their families back to their old village on Lost River, just above Tule Lake. Another group under a sub-chief, Hooker Jim, followed and camped on the opposite side of the river.

Settlers who now claimed all the land formerly occupied by the Modocs complained at once to the government authorities. The usual conferences, reports, and postponements of action followed until the autumn of 1872, when the Indian agent at Fort Klamath received a telegram ordering him to proceed to Lost River and return the Modoc Indians to the Klamath reservation.

A final council was held on November 27, 1872, but Captain Jack refused to discuss returning to the reservation. He insisted that the Modocs be given a reservation in their own country, and he was sustained in his plea by Brigadier General Edward R. S. Canby, who was then commanding the Department of the Pacific. The General was overruled by higher authority, however, and at dawn on November 29, 1872, Major James Jackson led a cavalry detachment of thirty-six men into the Modoc camp with orders to force the Modocs to return to Klamath.

The Indians' dogs were barking loudly as the soldiers rode directly up to the chief's lodge, halted, and dismounted. Captain Jack's head man, Scarface Charley, was ordered to bring the chief outside. When Jack appeared from his lodge, he was carrying his gun, and from out of the darkness his braves appeared, also well-armed.

Major Jackson informed the Modocs that he had been sent to take them back to the reservation. "I will go," Captain Jack replied, "but why do you come to my camp when it is dark?"

The cavalry commander assured Jack that he did not seek to do harm to his people. Then he added, pointing to a bunch of sagebrush: "Lay your gun down over there."

"What for?" asked Jack.

"You are the chief. You lay your gun down, all your men do the same."

After considering the order for a few moments, Captain Jack signaled to his men to disarm themselves. But when Scarface Charley refused to give up his pistol, an argument followed. In a few seconds, Indians and soldiers were firing at each other. Eight soldiers and fifteen of the Modocs were killed in the close-range action.

Though he had repeatedly said that he had not wanted a war with the white men, Captain Jack knew that he now had one on his hands. He certainly must have considered the possibility of a war, and had plan-

General Edward R. S. Canby. Canby, commander of the U. S. Army's Department of the Pacific, believed the Modocs should be given a reservation in their own country rather than return to the Klamath reservation which they had fled in 1870. The General was overruled by Washington authorities, however, and on November 29, 1872, a cavalry detachment was sent to Captain Jack's camp to force the Modocs to go back.

Scarface Charley. When a cavalry commander ordered the Modocs to surrender their arms, Captain Jack's head man, Scarface Charley, refused. In the argument that followed, Charley fired off his pistol, precipitating a skirmish in which eight soldiers and fifteen Modocs were killed.

162

ned a strategy to meet it. The Modocs moved swiftly to the Lava Beds south of Tule Lake. They could have selected no better defensive position anywhere than among the caves and rocks and secret passages of this jagged volcanic mass. And when Jack and his band reached the Lava Beds, they were reinforced by Hooker Jim and his followers, who had been attacked by civilian volunteers on their side of the river. In retaliation, Hooker Jim's Modocs had slain several settlers on the flight to the Lava Beds.

The war was on in earnest, and volunteer companies were organized as rapidly as the news spread through Oregon and California. But it was mid-January before the First Cavalry, the Twenty-first Infantry, and the volunteers were ready to attack the formidable defenses of the Lava Beds. They numbered four hundred men; the Modocs had seventy-five warriors and one hundred fifty women and children.

Under the cover of a dense morning fog, an attack was launched on January 17, 1873. The combatants could not see each other, could only fire blindly at orange-colored flashes of gunfire. The voices of the Indians echoing mockingly, and the fog curling over the wet fantastic shapes of the rocks added to the weirdness of the battle. Although the troops brought up a howitzer battery and fired all through the day, they were forced to retire at nightfall. Sixteen men were dead, fifty-three wounded. The Modocs had not lost a man.

General Canby now took personal command, bringing in reinforcements, raising his strength to a thousand men. He was striving vainly to reach the Modocs with mortars when Washington suddenly ordered a halt to the costly fighting, and arrangements were begun for a peace parley.

Through Princess Winema, a relative of Captain Jack, the government authorities were able to approach the besieged Modocs. Winema had married Frank Riddle, a miner from Kentucky, and she had adopted her husband's civilization, even changing her

The Lava Beds. With a war on their hands, the Modocs moved to the Lava Beds south of Tule Lake. The caves and secret passages of these jagged volcanic rocks provided superb defensive positions.

name to Tobey Riddle. The Riddles offered their services as intermediaries to General Canby, and on February 28, they went with Elisha Steele and two other old friends of Captain Jack to arrange a parley.

Although the Modocs were split into two factions, Hooker Jim and Schonchin John insisting on a war to the death, Captain Jack finally agreed to a discussion. Alfred B. Meacham, a Quaker who had a reputation for fairness to the Indians, was appointed head of the peace commission. With General Canby and Reverend Eleazer Thomas, Commissioner Meacham went to meet the Modocs in the Lava Beds on March 27. Very little was accomplished at this meeting. Captain Jack parried most of their remarks by continually referring to previous broken promises and ill-treatment of his people. "I am sorry to say I cannot trust these men that wear blue cloth and brass buttons," he said. The council was ended with handshakes, however, and Jack promised to talk with them again at a later date.

During the next two weeks, the breach between Captain Jack and Hooker Jim grew wider. Schonchin John insisted on a war council, and accused Jack of having less courage than a "fish-hearted woman." Schonchin John then bragged that he would take it upon himself to kill General Canby, and with Hooker Jim, he succeeded in working the Modocs up to the frenzy of a war dance. They were singing war chants the day before the next meeting with the peace commission.

Winema warned General Canby and Commissioner Meacham not to return to the Lava Beds. She had heard that Captain Jack had agreed to participate in a plot to kill all the members of the commission. General Canby, however, refused to believe that the Modocs would dare to do this, at least not while he had a thousand soldiers drawn up around the Lava Beds.

On the morning of April 11, Canby, Meacham, Thomas, Frank and Tobey Riddle, L. S. Dyer, the Klamath agent, all mounted horses and rode off for

Picket Station. On January 17, 1873, under
cover of a dense morning fog, a force of cavalry
and infantry attacked the Modocs at the Lava
Beds. Visibility was poor, and after a day of
blind firing sixteen soldiers were dead, fifty-three
wounded. The Modocs had not lost a man.

Army Camp South of Tule Lake.   General Canby brought in reinforcements, raising his strength to a thousand men. He was trying vainly to reach the Modocs with mortar fire when the government suddenly ordered a halt to the costly fighting. Arrangements began for a peace parley.

Captain Jack's camp. It was a bright spring day with the sun shining warmly when they started, but by the time they reached the Modoc outpost, snow was flurrying out of heavy clouds that had gathered over the rocky landscape.

As soon as he reached Jack's campfire, General Canby held out a box of cigars to the chief and his men. The gifts were accepted with thanks, the Indians lighting them immediately with burning brands from the fire. The talk began slowly.

"My Modoc friends," said the General, "my heart feels good today. I feel good because you are my friends. We will do good today."

Jack puffed at his cigar. "General Canby, your law is as crooked as this." He held up a sagebrush twig. "The agreements you make are as crooked as this." He drew a wavy line in the dirt with his fingertip. "Take away your soldiers. Take away your big guns, and then we can talk peace."

Canby glanced at Meacham, and the commissioner spoke up quickly: "General Canby can't take the soldiers away without permission of the Great Father in Washington. If you will come out of the rocks and go with us, we promise to find a new home for the Modocs." As he was talking, Mecham noticed that Hooker Jim, who had been pacing nervously back and forth, had walked up to the commissioner's horse, had taken the overcoat from the saddle and was putting it on. Suddenly, Hooker Jim turned toward the council circle, buttoning up the huge overcoat. "Me Old Man Meacham now," he said, beating his breast and grinning.

Meacham, Canby, and the others laughed. The commissioner took off his hat and handed it to Hooker Jim. "You'd better take my hat, too, Jim," he said.

"No hurry," Hooker Jim replied slyly. "Will get hat by-n-by."

Captain Jack, meanwhile, had not even smiled. He was scratching designs in the hard earth with the

Schonchin John. Schonchin John, with Hooker Jim, created a split within the Modoc council, accusing Captain Jack of lacking courage in agreeing to a peace parley. They urged the Modocs to continue the war with Canby's forces, and John boasted that he would kill the General himself if Captain was afraid to do so. When a peace commission visited the Lava Beds on April 1, 1873, Captain Jack shot and killed Canby, thus ending all hope for peace.

sagebrush twig. "Tell me what you will do," he said to General Canby. "I am tired waiting for you to speak."

Meacham now realized that the situation was becoming dangerous. "Promise him something," he said in an undertone to the General. But before Canby could speak, Captain Jack jumped up and started walking away. Schonchin John glowered after his chief, then stepped into his place before the council fire. "You take away soldiers, you give us back land," he shouted. "We tired talking. We talk no more!"

As Schonchin John shouted out these words, Captain Jack swung around and cried in Modoc: "*Ot-we-kau-tux-e* (Let us do it, or All ready!)"

The circle of Indians around the white men closed in quickly, revolvers and rifles ready. Canby stared at Captain Jack, who was pointing a pistol directly at him. The hammer clicked on a dead cartridge. A second later, the trigger clicked again, and this time Canby was hit. A Modoc named Boston Charley had shot Thomas at almost the same moment. Winema, meanwhile, had saved Meacham's life by knocking Schonchin John's pistol to one side. Meacham was wounded, and Boston Charley tried to scalp him, but Winema interceded and was able to get the commissioner to safety. Frank Riddle and Dyer also escaped.

Thus ended all hopes for peace. The commander of the Department of the Columbia, Colonel J. C. Davis, replaced Canby, and after days of terrific artillery bombardments, the Modocs surrendered. Hooker Jim quit first, hoping to escape punishment for his part in the war. After a wild foot race across the rocks and through a thicket, Captain Jack was captured alone on May 31.

He came out of the brush, brazenly wearing General Canby's blue uniform, now dirty and in tatters. "Jack's legs gave out," he said. "I am ready to die." This was the end of the "most costly war in which the U. S. ever engaged, considering the number of opponents," the end of what Hubert H. Bancroft called

Princess Winema. Princess Winema, cousin
of Captain Jack, offered her services as
intermediary in a peace parley between
General Canby and Captain Jack.

171

Schonchin John and Captain Jack in Chains.
After days of terrific artillery bombardment,
Hooker Jim, Schonchin, and then Captain
Jack surrendered. The Modoc leaders were
hanged in October, 1873.

"a brave and stubborn fight for native land and liberty—a war in some respects the most remarkable that ever occurred in the history of aboriginal extermination."

The Modoc leaders were taken to Klamath reservation and placed in jail. In October, Captain Jack, Schonchin John, Black Jim, and Boston Charley were hanged. During his last moments, a minister came to comfort Captain Jack. The chief received the visitor politely. "You say, Mr. Preacher, that the place I am going to is a nice place. Do you like this place you call Heaven?"

The minister replied that Heaven was a beautiful place.

"Well," Jack continued, without a change of tone or expression, "I tell you what I will do. I give you twenty-five head of ponies if you take my place today, as you say Heaven is such a nice place. Because I do not like to go right now."

The visitor declined Captain Jack's offer. The Modoc chief was hanged, his body preserved, and taken on a tour of the east where it was put on public exhibition, admission ten cents. The remnants of his Modoc band were exiled to Indian Territory.

Nez Percé Lodge. The Nez Percés lived north of the Modocs and northwest of the Sioux, in the valleys between the Blue and Bitter Root Mountains. They had developed a culture well above the level of other western tribes.

174

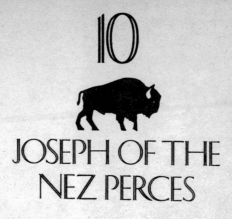

JOSEPH OF THE NEZ PERCES

FAR TO THE NORTH of the Modocs and northwest of the fighting Sioux lived one of the most advanced tribes of Indians in North America—the Nez Percés. In the beautiful valleys between the Blue and the Bitter Root Mountains, the Nez Percés had developed a culture that was above the usual nomadic level of other tribes of the West. They were a people of superior intelligence; they loved peace; and most of all, they loved their land.

In 1805, Lewis and Clark had found the Nez Percés to be friends. Later explorers, missionaries, and then the settlers were also treated as friends. When artist Alfred Jacob Miller visited the Nez Percés in 1839, he observed: "These Indians are anti-belligerent and have some other qualities that are rare and commendable." He added prophetically: "All these Indians seem to bear the impress of a doomed race."

At the time of Miller's visit, Dr. Marcus Whitman and the Reverend Henry Spalding were having great success in their efforts to found missions among the Nez Percés. From the numerous small bands of the tribe, three leaders, Kalkalshuatash, Tamason, and Tuekakas, were converted, changing their names respectively to Jason, Timothy, and Joseph.

Old Squaw. Nez Percé habits of life differed considerably from most of their neighbors. They fished for salmon, kept herds of horses, and gathered roots and berries in season. Above all, they loved their land.

Tamason. When Dr. Marcus Whitman and his missionaries arrived before 1850 they found the Nez Percé leaders eager and willing to abandon their old religion for the Christianity of the white men. Tamason became one of the first converts, changing his name to Timothy.

Within a few years, however, Joseph left the mission at Lapwai and led his band back to their old home in the Wallowa Valley. He did not like the talk of the men who came with the missionaries, the white settlers who wanted to buy the lands of the Nez Percés.

"The earth is our mother," said Joseph. "We cannot sell you our mother." And as the settlers became more insistent, Joseph's band adopted the philosophy of a prophet who called himself Smohalla. Smohalla the Preacher believed that the Indians must return to their primitive mode of life, and must reject the teachings and things of the white man.

Old Joseph's son, Young Joseph, also followed the teachings of Smohalla, and the second Joseph became the greatest of the Nez Percés, if not the greatest of all American Indians. As a young man, he had been for a time a student in one of the white man's schools. He had listened to his father, Old Joseph, plead with the white men, and he had seen many promises broken by them.

In 1855, when the invaders had demanded that Old Joseph move his tribe out of the Wallowa Valley, the chief had refused. He had not only refused to move, but he insisted that a definite line of demarcation between white man's territory and Nez Percé territory be drawn on the council map across the top of the Blue Mountains. The gold seekers and the land seekers, however, desired the Valley of Winding Waters for their exclusive use. Old Joseph was summoned to another council in 1859.

"The line was made as I wanted it," he told the commissioners this time. "Not for me, but for my children that will follow me. There is where I live, and there is where I want to leave my body. The land on the other side of the line," he concluded significantly, "is what we gave to the Great Father. Can you not leave us in peace in our valley?"

Young Joseph heard his father's remarks on this occasion and remembered them until the day he died. Was it possible that the white men wanted the Valley of Winding Waters in addition to all the other land the Indians had given them? He could scarcely believe this. But not long after Young Joseph became chief, his father warned him: "When you go into council with the white man, always remember your country. Do not give it away. The white man will cheat you out of your home. I have taken no pay from the United States. I have never sold our land."

In 1863, Young Joseph attended his first council as a chief. The Indian commissioners, acting under pressure from the settlers, had drawn up a treaty which removed to a reservation all the Nez Percés, including Joseph's band in the Wallowa Valley. Joseph, of course, refused to sign. He went back to his land, and warned all white men to keep out.

To avoid trouble, the government took no action against him, but cattle ranchers began grazing their

Smohalla and His Priests. About the year 1850, a religious prophet arose among the Nez Percés—Smohalla the Preacher. He taught that the Indians must cling to their primitive mode of life, refuse the teachings and things of the white man, and be guided by the will of God as revealed to Smohalla in dreams.

Joseph.   As a young man, Joseph, son of Tuekakas the original Joseph, attended many treaty councils with his father and learned how the white men broke their promises. In 1863, having become the leader of his tribe, he attended his first council as a chief. He refused to sign a treaty that would have removed his people from their beautiful Wallowa Valley, the Valley of Winding Waters.

179

herds over Joseph's land, using pastures which the Nez Percés needed for their cattle and ponies. More gold also had been discovered at Orofino, and the miners were coming in droves.

In 1868, Timothy and Jason with other leaders who wanted to follow the white man's way, traveled to Washington to sign a treaty. As heads of the Nez Percés, they agreed to withdraw the entire tribe to a reservation. Chief Joseph, however, did not go to Washington, signed no treaty, and ignored all orders to move from Wallowa Valley. The Office of Indian Affairs finally sent an agent to interview Joseph in 1873, and as a result of this meeting, the Secretary of the Interior decided that the Wallowa Valley was rightfully the property of the Nez Percés. On June 16, 1873, President Ulysses S. Grant issued an order:

"It is hereby ordered that the tract of country described be withheld from entry and settlement as public lands, and that the same be set apart as a reservation for the roaming Nez Percés, as recommended by the Secretary of Interior and the Commissioner of Indian Affairs."

This turn of events brought joy to the hearts of Joseph and his people; at last, the Great Father had recognized their claim. The settlers, however, so resented the government's action that they threatened openly to exterminate all the Nez Percés in the valley. Telegraph wires across the continent hummed with indignant demands. Joseph wisely began gathering as many allies as he could: his brother Alikut; an influential disciple of Smohalla, Tu-hul-hil-sote; and two chieftains, White Bird and Looking Glass. While he was doing this, the army was sending troops into the neighboring areas.

The tension lasted for almost two years. Then the Nez Percés were dismayed to learn that President Grant had suddenly reversed his order. All their beautiful valley was to be opened to white settlers! In the spring of 1875, General O. O. Howard, commander of the Department of the Columbia, met

Jason. Jason, with Timothy and other leaders, traveled to Washington in 1868 to sign a treaty removing all Nez Percés to reservations. Chief Joseph, refusing to abide by a treaty he had not signed, kept his loyal band in the Wallowa Valley.

General O. O. Howard. In 1875 the government opened the Valley of Winding Waters to legal settlement and ordered the Nez Percés to move to Lapwai reservation in Idaho. It was the duty of General Howard, commander of the Department of the Columbia, to enforce this order. The General protested to Washington, but the authorities had made up their minds.

Joseph near Pendleton, Oregon. Howard reported to Washington: "I think it is a great mistake to take from Joseph and his band of Nez Percés Indians that valley. Possibly Congress can be induced to let these really peaceable Indians have this poor valley for their own." But the government took no further action. Violent incidents began to occur here and there in the valley, and General Howard sent more troops to keep the peace.

Joseph and the General met for the second time in 1876. An Indian commission was present, and once again they asked Joseph why he refused to move to the Lapwai reservation with the other Nez Percés.

"I have not come to talk about my land," he replied. "For many years my father and I have talked about our land to the whites. They will not listen. It is still our land, but the whites will not stay off it."

General Howard asked him another question: "Suppose several thousand men should come from Oregon with arms, what would you do?"

Joseph was silent for a moment, then spoke as if choosing his words carefully: "The white settlers are bad enough. Your soldiers are worse. We have seen them paraded around this whole country. Three or four times they have come into the Wallowa as if to tell us they would make war at any time. We always lived at peace until the white man came. We have not made any war on the white man. But they have pushed over the limits my father set up. They have come over the limits Governor Stevens set up. Now, if soldiers come, what will we do? We will not sell the land. We will not give up the land. We love the land; it is our home."

The commission's reply was direct: "Unless they come to Lapwai and settle in a reasonable time, they are to be placed by force upon the reservation." Joseph was formally notified that he had until April 1, 1877, to come on the reservation peaceably. When the Nez Percés ignored the order, General Howard went to see Joseph. All the allied chiefs came to the council,

Tu-hul-hil-sote, Looking Glass, and White Bird. After long discussions, Joseph and his fellow chieftains decided they would have to bow to the power of the white men.

Yet in June, when they started the long march to Lapwai from the Wallowa, White Bird, Tu-hul-hil-sote, and Alikut began to speak for war. Joseph told them it was "better to live at peace than to begin a war and lie dead." The others called him a coward. One night a few irresponsible braves, unknown to Joseph, went on a raid. Within a few days, death was riding in the valleys of the Salmon and the Snake. Eleven white men and thirty-three Nez Percés were killed the first week. In spite of Joseph's efforts, the war he had feared for so long had now begun.

Though he had opposed the war, now that it had come Joseph was regarded by all as the leader. Without hesitation he began preparing his defenses. The lodges of the Nez Percés were struck, and the seven hundred men, women, and children moved up to the comparative safety of White Bird Creek. Joseph's wife was expecting a child, and after the custom of the tribe, he pitched their tipi to one side of the camp. Pickets were posted at the entrance of White Bird Canyon, and the Nez Percés waited the coming of the white man's soldiers.

The troops of the First Cavalry under Colonel David Perry entered the canyon at dawn on June 17. Through the narrow passage, the soldiers could see the white gleam of the Salmon River. As the darkness lifted, two columns of smoke were visible above the Indian encampment. Perry thought he had trapped Joseph, but he did not know that he was dealing with a master strategist.

While the cavalrymen were approaching along the winding floor of the canyon, Joseph sent White Bird with a large force into concealment along one side of the defile. When the troops reached the opening into the valley, Joseph and his warriors sprang up and began a fierce attack, distracting the soldiers until

Ready for the Great March. En route to the Lapwai reservation, a group of militant Nez Percé warriors left the marching party and began to raid settlers in the Salmon and Snake valleys. And thus war began, and the long tragic flight of the Nez Percés. They could not follow the examples of other tribes and retreat westward—there was no "west" for them—and so they headed north toward Canada. (This photograph, made some years after, includes several participants of the march.)

White Bird could swing down from the left and turn Perry's flank. In a few minutes, the cavalrymen were routed, cut into indefensible pockets. A third of the troops were killed before they could escape in disorder through the canyon's mouth. Even after they had re-formed, they could not make a stand. Joseph drove the soldiers almost to the town of Mt. Idaho, then ordered his warriors back to the safety of the camp. "Take weapons and ammunition," he said, "but no scalps."

When he returned to his tipi, he found that his wife had given birth to a girl child. He wondered how long it would be until the white men came again.

Ten days later, his scouts brought the news that General Howard was marching from Lapwai with very large forces. With the cunning of a fox, Joseph waited until the General was almost into the Salmon

Valley. Then he crossed the mountains, forcing Howard to divide his army. In a succession of masterful moves, the Indian completely out-maneuvered the veteran military commander, almost wiped out one of the pursuing detachments, and raced to the Clearwater where Looking Glass was waiting with a new force of warriors.

Now that he had almost three hundred warriors armed with rifles, Joseph decided to attack Howard boldly as soon as the four hundred soldiers were in striking range. Incredible as it may seem, Joseph was again successful, outflanking the General and cutting his communications. If cavalry reinforcements had not come up from Lapwai, this might have been Howard's last battle.

Withdrawing beyond the Clearwater, Joseph called a council of the chiefs—White Bird, Looking Glass, and Alikut. They all knew that they could never hope to return again to their beloved valley. They were already outnumbered eight to one, and more soldiers would be coming from the east. Only one course was left to them—flight to Canada. Sitting Bull of the Sioux had escaped to Canada, and the white soldiers dared not go there to capture him. If the Nez Percés could reach the Lolo Trail and cross the Bitter Root Mountains, perhaps they might be able to reach the northern country.

Although Howard guessed what the chiefs were planning and sent a detachment to block the Lolo Trail, the Indians cleverly outwitted the small force and crossed successfully into Montana. Here Joseph faced his greatest problem. He could not risk crossing the open plains of Montana which were dotted with military posts. And the northern route was blocked by Howard's troops.

To escape to Canada, he was forced to turn south along the chain of mountains, hoping to shake off his pursuers. His uncanny knowledge of the geography of this vast area amazed the officers who were trying vainly to trap him.

Not until they reached the Big Hole did the Nez Percés meet trouble. Here General Gibbon, coming in from Montana on the night of August 9, caught the weary Indians asleep in camp. More women and children than warriors were slain in this dawn attack. After the first shock of the assault, Joseph rallied his fighting men and they drove Gibbon back, capturing one of his howitzers and two thousand rounds of ammunition. But Looking Glass had died early in the battle.

Howard had now almost overtaken the fleeing tribe. After a brief skirmish at Camas Meadows, however, the Nez Percés escaped again, by cutting across the Yellowstone. Hopefully they turned north into Montana—only to face a new disaster. A fresh force of Seventh Cavalry troops under Colonel Samuel Sturgis from Fort Keogh blocked them at Canyon Creek.

It was September now, and the nights were bitter cold. Canada was still many miles away. Desperately, Joseph once again ordered his thinning line of warriors into battle. After two days' fighting, Sturgis' forces were completely scattered, but there were not many fighting braves left alive.

The survivors had one more chance. They moved swiftly northward. General Nelson Miles with a large force of cavalry was racing to cut them off. Only thirty miles from the Canadian border, in the Bear Paw Mountains, the last battle was joined. Snow was falling when Miles attacked on September 30, but the Indians fought back with desperate fury.

Surrounding Joseph's camp, Miles demanded unconditional surrender. The Nez Percés held out until October 5, when a second blizzard swept across the mountains. "I could not bear to see my wounded men and women suffer any longer," Joseph said afterward. When he rode out to meet General Howard, who had joined Miles, Joseph was holding his rifle loosely across his thighs, both hands clasped on his saddle pommel. He dismounted from his horse with dignity, handing his gun to the General.

"I am tired of fighting," he said. "Our chiefs are killed. Looking Glass is dead. Tu-hul-hil-sote is dead. The old men are all dead. He who led on the young men, Alikut, is dead. It is cold and we have no blankets. The little children are freezing to death. My people, some of them, have run away to the hills, and have no blankets, no food; no one knows where they are —perhaps freezing to death. I want to have time to look for my children and see how many of them I can find. Maybe I shall find them among the dead. Hear me, my chiefs. I am tired; my heart is sick and sad. From where the sun now stands I will fight no more forever."

The long journey was ended. After a thousand miles of fighting, only eighty-seven warriors were now alive, and half of them were wounded. Joseph's wife was dead, his older daughter had escaped to Canada with

The Pursuers. Soldiers came from all directions in pursuit of the Nez Percés. At White Bird Canyon, Joseph won his first battle. At Clearwater, he outmaneuvered General Howard's vastly superior forces. After surviving a surprise attack at Big Hole and a skirmish at Camas Meadows, Joseph turned south into the wilds of the Yellowstone. But at Canyon Creek, the Seventh Cavalry finally blocked him.

Looking Glass. Looking Glass, Joseph's ablest lieutenant, died in the battle of the Big Hole. Weary from days of continuous marching, their horses gone, and outnumbered eight to one, the Nez Percés somehow rallied and captured a howitzer and two thousand rounds of ammunition. But they had lost their best warriors and many women and children.

Surrender. Only thirty miles from Canada in the Bear Paw Mountains, his people exhausted by hunger and bitter cold weather, Joseph surrendered unconditionally to General Miles on October 5, 1877.

White Bird, and only the girl papoose born on the flight was left to him. But he hoped that the remnants of his tribe would now be left in peace on the Lapwai reservation.

This was not to be, however. Orders came from Washington to remove the Nez Percés to Fort Leavenworth, Kansas. Joseph's protests went unheeded. He and his people were floated on flatboats

Joseph's Final Home, Nespelem, Washington.
After surrendering, the Nez Percés were transported in freight cars to the hot plains of Indian Territory in Kansas, where many of them died. Finally, in 1885, Joseph was transferred to Colville reservation in the state of Washington, where he died in 1904.

down the Missouri River to a malarious bottomland where they were cooped up during the winter of 1877–78. Accustomed to mountain water and air, one-fourth of the Nez Percés sickened and died in this new country.

In the heat of the following summer, those who survived were crowded into railroad freight cars and transported to Indian Territory. Suffering from desert heat and ill with nostalgia for the clean winds of the Valley of Winding Waters, they died one by one.

Bureaucrats and Christian gentlemen visited Joseph at intervals during the following years, interviewing him and making endless reports to their various organizations. Joseph was even allowed to visit Washington, but government officials by this time were bored by touring chiefs, and scarcely any attention was paid to his pleas. Finally, a small group of "good" Nez Percés were permitted to return to Lapwai. Then in 1885, Joseph was transferred to Nespelem on the Colville reservation in the state of Washington.

Although he was back in the northwest, he was still an exile from the valley of his fathers. When he fell suddenly dead one autumn day in 1904, his friends said that he had died of a broken heart.

Ocheo's Wickiup.   The Paiutes, who inhabited the country around
Pyramid Lake in Nevada, lived in wickiups, small rounded huts of tule
rushes fastened over frameworks of poles, with the ground for a floor
and a fire in the center.

192

THE PEACE SEEKERS

I

DURING THE FLOW of migration westward to the Pacific coast, some of the Indian tribes escaped conflict with the white men through the skillful efforts of their leaders. Such were the Paiutes, the Utes, and the Shoshones. Their outstanding leaders were Chief Winnemucca and his granddaughter Sarah Winnemucca, Ouray the Arrow, and Washakie of the Shoshones.

Old Chief Winnemucca was the outstanding chieftain among the Paiute bands that made their homes around Pyramid Lake in Nevada. When John C. Fremont journeyed through that section in 1845, he and Winnemucca became good friends, and the chief agreed to accompany the exploring party as a guide across the mountains to California.

Winnemucca liked the white man's country along the coast, and when he returned to Pyramid Lake and found that he had become the grandfather of a girl papoose, he resolved to have her educated in California schools. And so before he died in 1859, the old chief arranged for his granddaughter, Tocmetone, to attend a mission school at San Jose. This was the beginning of her career as a peacemaker between the Paiutes and the white men.

As soon as she learned to speak and write English,

Tocmetone changed her name to Sarah Winnemucca, a name which was to become more famed than that of her grandfather.

During the Sixties, there were frequent clashes between the Nevada tribes and the new settlers. Apparently the Younger Winnemucca lacked the qualities of leadership that his father had possessed. He was a chief in name only, and was having difficulty restraining his angry warriors from going on the warpath, when Sarah Winnemucca returned from California filled with a desire to help her father's people adjust to their changing environment.

As she was able to speak both English and Paiute, Sarah became an interpreter. By winning the friendship of Nevada's Governor James W. Nye, she also won many concessions for her people. But inevitably, the pressure from the miners, the settlers, and the overland stage companies forced the authorities to transfer the Paiutes north to the state of Oregon to be quartered on Malheur Reservation.

Sarah Winnemucca, meanwhile, had married a Lieutenant Bartlett, who had been stationed at Fort McDermit, Nevada. When Bartlett was dismissed from the service and departed for the east, Sarah followed her father's band of Paiutes to Malheur and became a school teacher there.

For several years she worked earnestly to improve the condition of the Indians, but the corruption of the agency officials finally led her to plan a visit to Washington where she hoped to present her case before the highest authorities. She had traveled as far as Camp Lyon, Idaho, when she received news that the Paiutes had suddenly left Malheur Reservation to join the Bannocks.

The Bannock Indians, led by Buffalo Horn, had previously departed their reservation and returned to the Camas Prairie of southern Idaho, where they were holding war dances and collecting stolen horses and weapons to drive out the settlers. Seeking allies among the tribes in nearby reservations, Buffalo Horn had

194

The Winnemucca Family. Chief Winnemucca
and his daughter Sarah kept their Paiute
tribe at peace with the emigrants moving
westward to the Pacific coast. As she could
speak both English and Paiute, Sarah was
even more influential than her father in
helping these Nevada Indians to benefit from
their association with the white people. (*Left
to right:* Sarah Winnemucca, Chief
Winnemucca, Natchez, Captain Jim, an
unidentified boy.)

found willing listeners among the Paiutes at Malheur. In spite of the Younger Winnemucca's protests, the braves of his band went to join the Bannocks, forcing their unwilling chief to go with them.

Realizing that her people were doomed to destruction as soon as General O. O. Howard could gather his armies, Sarah Winnemucca hurried to Silver City, where she found Captain Reuben F. Bernard in charge of Howard's first attacking force. She persuaded Captain Bernard to hold off his fight with the Bannocks until she had made an attempt to bring the Paiutes out of Buffalo Horn's camp. "The people of Winnemucca do not wish to fight the soldiers," she declared.

Under cover of darkness, she approached the Bannock encampment, and by chance met one of her brothers, Lee Winnemucca. He agreed with Sarah that the Paiutes should withdraw from their alliance with the bellicose Bannocks. He suggested that she exchange her usual neat dress for a squaw's blanket, and together they crept into the camp, found their father, and led most of the Paiute warriors away before the Bannocks knew what was happening.

"Princess" Sarah Winnemucca remained with General Howard's staff for the remainder of the Bannock campaign, serving as a scout and interpreter. Afterwards, she and her father traveled in the east where she lectured and wrote articles and a book about her people. She was married for the second time in 1882, to a Lieutenant Hopkins. When he contracted tuberculosis, she took him back to Nevada where she bought a tract of land near Lovelock and opened a school for Indian children.

When Hopkins died in 1886, Sarah Winnemucca abandoned her school and her career, and finished out her life penuriously near the village of Monida, Montana.

The Bannocks Wanted War. The Paiutes
moved eventually to Malheur reservation in
Oregon. The Bannock Indians, who had fled
their reservation and now lived near the
Paiutes, persuaded some of the Paiutes to
join them in preparing for a war to drive out
the white settlers. Chief Winnemucca was
practically forced by his own warriors to join
the Bannock war camp, but war was averted
by the quick intercession of Sarah
Winnemucca.

197

II

Ouray the Arrow was the chief of the Uncompahgre
Utes of Colorado, a chief by virtue of inheritance
rather than by prowess in battle. Ouray preferred talking to fighting. He liked to talk so well that he learned
both English and Spanish, and would sit for hours
conversing with any traveler who might stop to listen.
After Ouray joined the Methodist Church, he discon-
tinued using profanity along with hard liquor and to-
bacco, but even under these self-imposed handicaps to
loquacity, he was known far and wide as an accomplished conversationalist.

Ouray's dislike for battle may have arisen as the
result of an encounter with the Sioux about 1860. In
this fight he lost his only son. Thereafter he was a man
of peace.

In 1862, he settled down on the Los Piños agency,
earning what was then a comfortable salary of five
hundred dollars per year as an official government interpreter. The Utes, meanwhile, were scattering all
over Colorado, and were being blamed for most of the
Indian trouble in the Rocky Mountain region.

To bring these wandering bands together, the government officials recognized Ouray as chief of all the
Utes, drew up a treaty at Conejos on October 7, 1863,
and assigned land and hunting ground boundaries to
the tribe. The garrulous chief thus suddenly became a
man of power and affluence.

The Utes had long been friends of Kit Carson, and
when the old scout came to Colorado after the Sand
Creek massacre of 1864, he and Ouray became in-
separable companions. The massacre of Black Kettle's Cheyennes had created a dangerous situation
in the gold country, and Carson's unofficial assign-
ment was to act as a peacemaker and moulder of
treaties.

Ouray, who looked upon Carson as something of a

god, was of considerable assistance to the scout in helping to quiet the rebellious Indians. In turn, when Ouray wanted to suppress an uprising led by a sub-chief, Kaniatse, Carson volunteered to assist in the action. Afterwards they went to Washington together on a treaty junket, a journey which must have been a continual round of tale-spinning, as Kit Carson was as magnificent a talker as Ouray.

The chief's prestige among his people was lowered in 1872, however, when an attempt was made by the government to recover a large portion of the land given to the Utes in the Treaty of 1863. Resisting at first, Ouray suddenly changed his mind and signed away the territory. As soon as the Utes discovered that Ouray had received a thousand dollars per year for life and a fine farm and a house, in exchange for giving away their hunting grounds, they accused him of betraying his deer-hunting brothers.

An indirect result of this disillusionment was the Ute War of 1879. When hostilities flared up on the

Jack and Douglas. When chief Ouray signed away a large portion of Ute territory to the government, the Utes lost most of their deer-hunting grounds, which contributed to the outbreak of hostilities at the White River reservation. Two sub-chiefs, Jack (left) and Douglas, led a rebellion against Agent Nathan C. Meeker's orders to plow the fields and raise crops.

White River reservation, Ouray commanded the warriors to come in and surrender their arms. Instead of obeying, the angry Utes attacked a troop of cavalry, killed Major Thomas Thornburgh and a number of his command. They then swarmed upon the buildings of the agency to massacre Agent Nathan C. Meeker and his men and to carry off Mrs. Meeker and her daughter.

The fury of the Utes had been aroused by the policies of Meeker, an eccentric experimentalist who had come out to Colorado some years earlier to found a cooperative community at Greeley. He developed a set of theories on how to "civilize" the Indians, and had found an opportunity to test his ideas in 1878 when he was appointed agent at the White River reservation. "I propose to cut every Indian to bare starvation point if he will not work," announced Meeker enthusiastically. The Utes, who had been feeding and clothing themselves on the products of their hunting trips, did not find it easy to obey the strong-willed Meeker, who ordered them to move into log cabins and plow the fields and raise crops. When Meeker started playing off two chiefs, Jack and Douglas, one against the other, he was setting his own death trap.

It was Douglas who led the massacre. Meeker was shot down in his living room, dragged into the courtyard, and staked to the ground with an iron tent pole.

Ouray, the peacemaker, was powerless to stop the war, and the Utes were driven back to the fastnesses of the Roan Mountains of Utah. It was here in a desolate wasteland that the deerhunters finally were locked upon a reservation named for their chief.

But Ouray did not go there to join his people. He who preferred talking to fighting stayed on his comfortable Colorado farm until he died like a white man in 1880.

Ouray and Chipeta. As a result of the Ute War of 1879, the Utes were driven into the Roan Mountains of Utah. There, in a desolate wasteland, the deer hunters finally were locked upon a reservation named for Chief Ouray. But Ouray did not go to join his people. He remained with his wife, Chipeta, on his comfortable Colorado farm, given to him by the U. S. government. He died there in 1880.

Since the days of the Lewis and Clark expedition, the Shoshones had always been proud of their friendship with the white men. Sacajawea, the legendary Shoshone woman, had accompanied the explorers westward from Fort Mandan on the Missouri to her people's country beyond the Rockies.

In the same winter that Sacajawea went with Lewis and Clark through the mountain passes, there was born among the eastern Shoshones of Montana a boy child called Shoots Straight. When he was old enough to kill his first buffalo, Shoots Straight made from the skin of that animal's pate a rattle filled with stones which he kept as a charm. And from that time his people called him Washakie, "The Rattler."

As a young man, Washakie was a great warrior, leading the braves of his band in many battles against the Blackfeet and the Crows. By 1840, he was well known among the trappers, and the Hudson's Bay Company employed him seasonally as a guide in the Green River country of Wyoming.

During the peak of overland emigration following the opening of the Oregon Trail, Washakie ordered his followers to become friends with the white men. There are numerous accounts of amicable meetings between the travelers and the Shoshones, who went out of their way to help the wagon trains safely across fords. Though the emigrants' straying livestock often ruined the Indians' root and herding grounds, animals captured by any of Washakie's band were always dutifully returned to the rightful owners.

But by the spring of 1862, the Bannocks who lived in the same area were beginning to raid the smaller emigrant trains. Seeing the plunder that the Bannocks were obtaining with such ease, some of the Shoshones joined in the attacks. Washakie warned them. "You are all fools. You are blind and cannot see. You have no ears, for you do not hear. You are fools, for you do

Washakie. Washakie was light-skinned, very tall and handsome, a man of dignity. As early as 1840 he was working as a guide for the Hudson's Bay Company. When he became a leader of the Shoshones, he adopted the manners of a patriarch and was very fond of form and ceremony.

not understand. We can make a bow and arrows, but the white man's mind is strong and light.''

Taking his loyal followers to Fort Bridger, Washakie waited until General Patrick E. Connor had defeated the marauding Bannocks and Shoshones at Bear River. When the contrite survivors of this affair came in to Washakie's camp, the chief met them with cold dignity. He asked one of them: "Who are you?" The beaten Indian replied: "I am a Shoshone." Washakie shook his head and declared: "You have been whipped. Shoshones are never whipped. You are no Shoshone." The penitents, however, were taken back into the fold, Washakie believing that they had learned their lesson.

Not long afterwards, the Shoshones were given a reservation near Fort Bridger, and after the Sand Creek massacre of 1864, Washakie agreed to take the fleeing Arapahoes and Cheyennes. His Green River country was becoming a peaceful refuge.

But the white man's trails and telegraph lines and finally the hated railroads were swiftly ruining the once lush hunting grounds. Fearful of what his people might do if pressed too far, Washakie went to Agent Luther Mann at Fort Bridger and asked for a new reservation, off the routes of the western travelers. His reputation for peace and loyalty won for the Shoshones one of the most beautiful sections in Wyoming, the Wind River valley.

In 1868, the treaty was completed. When informed of its approval, the chief declared: "I am laughing because I am happy, because my heart is good. Now I see my friends are around me, and it is pleasant to meet and shake hands with them. You have heard what I want. The Wind River country is the one for me. I want for my home the valley of the Wind River and lands on its tributaries as far east as the Popoagie, and want the privilege of going over the mountains to hunt where I please."

Before the move was made, however, the chief chanced to overhear some of his younger braves argu-

Shoshones on Wind River. When the white man's telegraph lines and railroads sliced across the Shoshones' Green River hunting grounds, Washakie asked for a reservation away from the western travel-routes. In 1868 he was given the beautiful Wind River valley in Wyoming, and the Shoshones have lived there in peace to this day.

ing about his prowess as a warrior. Some of them said he was too old to remain as the chief of the mighty Shoshones. "He is too old to win victories in battle. He is an old woman who will not even scalp his victims. War blood no longer flows in his veins."

This talk angered Washakie, but he said nothing to the young bucks. He quietly disappeared for two moons, reappearing suddenly at the campfire one evening with seven scalps in his possession. He may have talked of peace with the white men, but the Blackfeet and the Crows were still his mortal enemies.

205

Washakie's Last Photograph. The Shoshones
staged dances for visitors and soldiers.
Washakie (*at left*) died soon after this photo was
taken. The Army ordered a military funeral,
the first ever given an Indian, and the procession
was the longest in the history of Wyoming.

"Let him who can do a greater feat than this claim the
chieftainship." he said, lifting the scalps above the
heads of the young braves. "Let him who would take
my place count as many scalps." His abilities as a
warrior were never questioned again.

After he became the undisputed ruler of the great
Wind River reservation, Washakie's policy was to
treat all Indians who warred against the white men as
his enemies.

At the time when General George Crook was preparing for the battle of the Rosebud, Washakie sent
eighty-six of his best scouts to assist the blue-coats.
Three weeks later he arrived himself, leading two
hundred warriors. When he arrived at Crook's headquarters, he was wearing a giant headdress of eagle

feathers sweeping far along the ground behind his pony's tail. The government, he said, had been generous to him. He would now show that the red man never forgot a kindness given.

As the years went by, he became a nationally known figure, a patriarch among the Indians of the West. He never allowed horse thieves or vagabonds to find refuge among his tribe. He became a devout Episcopalian, and tried to set what he thought was a correct moral example for his people.

When Washakie died in 1900, the Adjutant General of the U. S. Army ordered that he be given a military funeral, the first ever given to an Indian. The procession is said to have been the largest in the history of Wyoming, a mile and a half long, the mounted Indian police, the agency employees, the soldiers and officers of the U. S. Army, and all the Shoshones and Arapahoes of the reservation following behind the flag-draped casket.

In the granite of his monument were chiseled these words: Always Loyal to the Government and to His White Brothers.

Nachez. After the Apaches laid down their guns in 1873 and moved onto reservations, the people of Arizona began to forget their promises. The Apaches were forced to move from the choice lands originally marked off for them to the San Carlos Agency on the hot, dry flats of the Gila River. The boldest and wildest of the warriors, however, could not abide these indignities. Nachez, second son of the great Cochise, with fierce Victorio and like-minded tribesmen, fled south to the mountains of Chihuahua and Sonora. They raided Mexican cattle herds and supplied themselves with ammunition from Arizona and New Mexico citizens.

208

GERONIMO
AND CHIRICAHUAS

THE APACHE INDIANS subdued and settled on reservations by General George Crook in 1873, had not been allowed to walk the white man's road. (See Chapter 4.) No sooner did they lay down their rifles and pick up a hoe than the "Indian agents who had sought cover before came out, brave as sheep, and took charge of the agencies, and commenced their game of plundering."

One young agent, John P. Clum, tried subduing the warriors with kindness, but his methods were unpopular on the frontier. Clum was almost as much disliked as his Indian wards.

The greed of the white man for the spoils of Indian bounty, and the greed of the settlers for the richest land, brought about the removal of the Apaches from the homes promised them. They were forced to live on the hot, dry flats of the San Carlos.

Not all the Apaches moved to the new reservation. Many of them, especially the Chiricahua and Warm Springs bands, crossed the border into Mexico, into the mountains of Chihuahua and Sonora. Later, others from the reservation fled south and joined them.

These warriors, once led by Cochise and Mangas Coloradas, had lost none of their fighting qualities.

Victim. The renegade Apaches delighted in killing Mexicans—"with rocks," as they boasted.

Under new chiefs, Victorio and Nana of the Warm Springs band, Nachez and Chato of the Chiricahuas, they terrorized New Mexico and Arizona. They boasted of their killings, saying they fought Mexicans with rocks, not bullets.

In September, 1882, General Crook, whom the Apaches well remembered as the Grey Wolf Chief, returned to Arizona to take charge of his old wards. He went about the Territory with a guide and interpreter, talking with his old friends, finding out for himself what was wrong.

Alchise, a reservation chief, told him: "When you left, there were no bad Indians out. We were all content; everything was peace. The officers you had were all taken away, and new ones came in—a different kind. The good ones must all have been taken away, and the bad ones sent in their places. I have always been true, and obeyed orders. When the Indians broke out at San Carlos, when Major Randall was here, I helped him to go fight them. When Major Randall was here we were all happy, and we think of him yet. Oh, where is my friend Randall—the captain with the big mustache which he always pulled? He was my brother, and I think of him all the time."

The burden of complaint was the same from all the Apaches—Chalipun, Navatane, Santos, Chiquito, Ezkiminzin—all complained that they had been forced away from their homes, had been mistreated, and were not able to make a living at the San Carlos.

General Crook made a number of quick changes after his council with the Indians. The Apaches at San Carlos were permitted to scatter from the agency headquarters and settle on land of their own choosing on the reservation, by the creeks and springs, where they could raise crops and become self-supporting. They would wear identification tags, so that they could be recognized as reservation Indians, not renegades.

The assurance of peace on the reservation was coupled with preparations for war against the Apaches who had left. The pack trains were reorganized under Tom Moore. New Indian scouts were enlisted, and old guides and interpreters were re-hired. Al Sieber and Archie MacIntosh showed up again.

In March, 1883, the Apaches in Mexico set out on another raid. One band, under Geronimo, raided in Sonora for stock, while the other, led by Chato, swept through southern and central Arizona. Chato's band traveled four hundred miles in six days, killing twenty-six persons, and taking what ammunition they could pick up. One of Chato's party, Tsoe, known to the soldiers as "Peaches," a White Mountain Apache, deserted and surrendered himself at San Carlos. Peaches offered to guide General Crook to the hiding place of the Chiricahuas.

Final preparations were made for the campaign. An agreement had been arranged with the Mexican government permitting U. S. troops to cross the border when they were in pursuit of Indians, and this was what Crook intended to do—follow the renegades to their home *rancherias*.

The expedition, with Crook in command, set out

May 1, 1883, with one hundred ninety-three Apache scouts under Captain Emmet Crawford, and one company of the Sixth Cavalry, comprising forty-two enlisted men and two officers. There were field rations for sixty days, and one hundred fifty rounds of ammunition per man. Three hundred fifty pack mules carried the load. Before starting, the Apache scouts killed a couple of mules and sat to a feast of roast mule meat, a great treat.

By May 8, the command was in the heart of the wild Sierra Madre. Travel was done at night under the guidance of Peaches. The trail was rough, and several of the mules were lost over the cliffs.

One Apache camp was found, deserted. By this time the command was so close to the *rancherias* that the pack train was left behind while the scouts and troops moved forward on foot. On the fifteenth, the advance, Indian scouts under Crawford, surprised a camp belonging to Bonito and Chato. There was a short, sharp fight. Nine warriors were killed, and five Apache children captured. The rest of the Chiricahuas scattered into the wilderness.

Scouts. General Crook assured the reservation Indians they had nothing to fear. He would make war only on those who had fled the reservation. The friendly Apaches were recruited as scouts to help bring in their people.

The Apaches were tired of their mountain life. They were tired of being hunted; it was impossible to rest, for fear of surprise. They sent word into Crook's camp, offering to surrender and return to the reservation. Crook suggested that he did not care whether they surrendered or not—he would just as soon kill them all and be rid of them for good. Hearing this, the hostiles begged for peace, and it was granted. All the chiefs gave themselves up, Geronimo, Chato, Loco, Nachez the son of Cochise, and Kan-ti-no. Only Juh was missing. He had fled south, far up the Yaqui.

On May 24, the prisoners arrived at San Carlos. There were fifty-two men, and two hundred seventy-three women and children. Geronimo came in late. He stayed in the mountains with a few followers, stealing stock from the Mexicans, so that he should not return poor. He finally came in, in June, 1883, escorted by Lt. Britton Davis.

General Crook then arranged to have full control over the Apaches on the reservation. With a firm hand he helped them learn the ways of the white man. For two years there was no Indian trouble in Arizona or New Mexico. Chato and Geronimo had the best farms on the reservation.

II

Two years of peace made the agents brave again. The old troubles sprang up anew. There was quarreling and bickering between the soldiers and the agents over control of the Indians.

The Apaches were quick to see the friction between their two masters. Some of the chiefs were happy over it, for they knew a chance had come to regain some of their old power. Their medicine was stronger in the mountains than in the cornfields. Besides, had not this whole land once belonged to the Apache? He had been free, then, to go and do as he pleased.

The threatened outbreak of the restless ones oc-

Geronimo Comes In.   Crossing the border into
Mexico, a company of the Sixth Cavalry and
one hundred ninety-three Apache scouts pursued
the hostile Apaches. Fifteen days after
leaving San Bernardino Springs, the command
surprised a camp of Chiricahuas under Bonito
and Chato. The Apaches decided to surrender
and all the chiefs gave themselves up.
Geronimo (*left, mounted*) and Nachez (*with hat on*)
were among those who wanted to return
to San Carlos and peace. Geronimo's son
stands at his side; the warrior standing on the
right is unidentified.

214

curred on May 17, 1885. Nachez, Geronimo, Chihua-hua, Mangas, and one hundred forty followers fled the reservation. They traveled one hundred twenty miles without rest or food, and took refuge in the Black Range, New Mexico.

The soldiers followed immediately, helped by In-dian scouts, but it was soon evident that a major cam-paign would have to be organized, especially after the runaways crossed the border, back to their old fortress of the Sierra Madre. On September 5, the commands in the field were recalled, and General Crook, his headquarters at Fort Bowie, Arizona, commenced re-fitting his outfits for a new campaign.

By the end of November, two new commands under Britton Davis and Emmet Crawford had set out to hunt down the Apaches wherever they might be. Chato, once a feared and hunted warrior, was now a trusted scout with Crawford.

On January 10, 1886, Crawford and his scouts at-tacked the main camp of the Chiricahuas about ninety miles below Nacori, Sonora. The entire camp with all its plunder was taken, though none of the Apaches was captured.

The loss of their camp and equipment was enough to demoralize the Chiricahuas, so that Nachez, Chi-huahua, and Geronomo asked for a peace talk with Crawford. Before the talks took place, Crawford's camp of Indian scouts was attacked by Mexican troops, who thought all Apaches were fair game, peaceful or hostile.

Captain Crawford, attempting to stop the fight, was killed by a shot through the brain. Before the Mexi-cans could be made to understand that they were at-tacking United States troops, the commander of the Mexican force and fifteen of his soldiers had been killed. Lt. Marion P. Maus, aided by interpreter Tom Horn, finally stopped the fight.

The Chiricahuas, camped on a hill across from the scene of the fight, were "interested spectators." Later they had a council with Lt. Maus, and agreed to meet

215

The Restless One. Geronimo (*center*) soon realized that peace was not everything. His power in the mountains of Sonora had been greater than his influence in the cornfields of San Carlos reservation. He grew restless.

General Crook in "two moons," the exact time and place to be settled later, at their pleasure.

On March 16, Lt. Maus informed Crook that the Apaches were ready to talk peace. The General, with Captain John Bourke, Cyrus S. Roberts, and Roberts' young boy, Charlie, left Bowie for the council. An enterprising photographer from Tombstone, C. S. Fly, came along with his assistant and some equipment.

The Chiricahuas, fully rearmed and re-equipped after their fight with Crawford, had chosen a good spot for the peace talk, Cañon de los Embudos, Sonora, about twenty miles south of the border, near the Sonora-Chihuahua line.

The council began March 25, and lasted three days. Geronimo, who did most of the talking, was very nervous, and tried to show that he had left the reservation to escape arrest. General Crook called Geronimo

Mangas. Mangas, son of Mangas Coloradas, also disliked reservation life. In May, 1885, he, with Nachez, Geronimo, Chihuahua, and one hundred forty followers fled the San Carlos. The old life in Mexico, they decided, was better.

217

Surrender. The Chiricahuas finally held their peace talk with General Crook at Canon de los Embudos, Sonora, March 25 to 27, 1886. After much talk, the renegades surrendered on condition that they be sent east with their families for a few years, and then return to Arizona. (Geronimo is fourth from the left, seated; General Crook is second from the right, seated.)

a liar, saying he had broken his word so often he could not be trusted.

Alchise and Ka-e-ten-a, trusted Apache scouts, were sent to the Chiricahua camp to talk peace and divide opinion. They did their work well, and on the twenty-seventh both Nachez and Chihauhua were in favor of peace. Geronimo, seeing how things were going, also decided for peace. Crook promised that they would be sent east with their families for a few years, and then returned to Arizona.

No sooner had Crook started back to Fort Bowie, than a white man named Tribolet sold the Chiricahuas some whisky to celebrate the peace. The resulting drunk brought about a change of mind in Geronimo and Nachez. With twenty men and nineteen women and children they broke camp and fled south. Another campaign would be necessary to rout them out.

The result of this final outbreak was the resignation of General Crook from the Department of Arizona. His superiors in the east were not satisfied with the peace terms. They wanted unconditional surrender. They hinted, too, that the Indian scouts had been disloyal. General Crook knew that unconditional surrender would have driven the Chiricahuas back to the Sierra Madre, and he knew also that his scouts were loyal beyond question. But rather than operate with official disapproval, he resigned.

On April 7, the Chiricahuas who had surrendered left Bowie station on their way to exile in Florida. General Crook went to see them off. "There were seventy-seven in all of them—fifteen men, thirty-three women and twenty-nine children," he wrote, "it is a big relief to get rid of them." Four days later Crook left Arizona, and General Nelson A. Miles took command.

When Miles began his campaign, there were seventeen men and nineteen women and children left among the Chiricahuas who had fled. Miles decided to capture them in a new way—he would run them down with cavalry. Accordingly, he dismissed the Indian scouts, and set Captain H. W. Lawton, with cavalry, and mounted infantry after the Apaches south of the border.

The cavalry soon wore out, and became infantry. For three months, the commands chased the Chiricahuas in and out of Sonora while the wily warriors raided over wide areas in southern and central Arizona, killing settlers, stealing stock, and escaping all troops sent after them.

Finally, in July, 1886, Geronimo and Nachez let it be known that they would consider surrender if granted terms. Lt. Charles B. Gatewood, who had served under Crook and was well-known to the Chiricahuas, was recalled from his post at Fort Stanton, New Mexico, and sent out to talk peace. After a month of waiting, Geronimo allowed himself to be located, and the council took place. With considerable

Geronimo.   After the surrender to General Crook, the Apaches celebrated by getting drunk. While drunk, Geronimo and Nachez changed their minds, and with thirty-nine followers fled camp, going south into the mountains. It was for acts of this sort that Geronimo won his reputation as a great chief, though he actually was no chief. He was a good fighter and a daring leader, and attracted other warriors to him.

hesitation, Nachez and Geronimo took the advice of Gatewood and surrendered. The Apache war was over.

Not only were the runaway Chiricahuas sent to Florida exile, but also those who had remained on the reservation, and served faithfully as scouts. Their reward for services rendered was imprisonment along with those whose surrender they had helped to bring about.

Pressure from the Indian Rights Association and interested army people finally effected the removal of the Apaches to Mt. Vernon barracks, Alabama, and later to Indian Territory, where they live today.

En Route. When Geronimo and Nachez surrendered in September 1886 they were, with their entire band, sent into exile in Florida. Not only were the renegades sent away, but later *all* the Chiricahuas, even the faithful scout Chato, were sent east. The trainload of Apache prisoners was a curiosity in the east. Pictures were taken by enterprising photographers along the route.

Issue Day at Pine Ridge Agency, South Dakota, 1890. By 1889, the Indians of the West were all locked within the reservations. The Great White Father doled out food and clothing through his agents, and it was not necessary for one to prepare for the changes of the seasons.

The Dispossessed. The old days of the splendid hunts and the fighting were dead things of the past. The ceremonies of the tribes had become rituals without meaning. The great chiefs dreamed of the past, and after drinking the white man's crazy water, they would make big talk, but most of the time there was nothing to be done. (At Pine Ridge Agency. Tall man wearing hat in center is Buffalo Bill Cody. Others include Kicking Bear, Crow Dog, Short Bull, Young-Man-Afraid-of-His-Horses, American Horse, and Two Lance.)

13

THE GHOST DANCE AND WOUNDED KNEE

I

EVERYWHERE NOW the Indians of the West were locked within the reservations. The great chiefs were shorn of their power. Many of the mighty warriors were dead. Those who lived spent their days in idleness. The buffalo and the antelope had vanished; the old ceremonies of the tribes had become rituals without meaning. The Great White Father doled out food and clothing through his agents, and it was not necessary for one to think of the changes of the seasons, the moons of the snow and cold, the moons of greening grass, the moons when the buffalo bulls are fat, the moons of the ripening choke-cherries and the falling leaves.

There was nothing to be done. One might trade a few skins for the white man's crazy-water, and then it was possible to dream of the old days, the days of the splendid hunts and the fighting. They would drink the crazy-water and make big talk for a little while. But it was a time without spirit, a time of despair.

And in this time the medicine men became the leaders. Everywhere there were dreamers and swooning men. Most of them were great fakers, but some were sincere in their vagaries and their visions.

Long before the Indians suffered their last great defeats, Smohalla the Prophet had preached his visions to the Nez Percés, and he had won the loyalty of Chief Joseph. When the Great Spirit had decided to make men on the earth, said Smohalla, he had made the Indians first. Then he had made the other peoples of the earth, but he was fast becoming dissatisfied with these other ones. That was why the Indians must not follow the ways of the white men.

Among the Apaches there had also been great dreamers. In 1881, Nakai-Doklini was teaching his followers in southern Arizona a new dance which he was certain would drive the whites from the land.

In Montana, a Crow medicine man, Sword Bearer, was preaching the same philosophy a few years later. He claimed that he was immune to bullets and weapons, and would soon make the hearts of the white men like water, so that they would go back to their homes in the east.

It was a time of despair, and in such time new religions are born. Why the religion reached its flower in Nevada and among the Paiutes, no one can say. But here it had begun in a small valley near the Walker River reservation south of Virginia City; here it had begun like the small trickle of a spring in the year 1870.

Tavibo, a petty chief, had made a lone pilgrimage into the mountains, and the divine spirits had made a revelation to him. All the people of the earth were to be swallowed up, he was told, but at the end of three days, the Indians would be resurrected in the flesh to live forever. They would enjoy the earth which was rightfully theirs. Once again there would be plenty of game, fish, and piñon nuts. Best of all, the whites would be destroyed forever.

When Tavibo reported his vision to the Mason Valley Paiutes, he attracted few believers. But gradually he added other features to his story, and he went up into the mountains again for further revelations. It was necessary for the Indians to dance, everywhere; to keep on dancing. This would please the Great Spirit, and in the Moon of the Little Grass, he would come and destroy the white men and bring back the game as thick as the stars in the Road of the Ghosts, the Milky Way.

Tavibo died shortly after he told of these things, but his son, Wovoka, was considered the natural inheritor of his powers by those Paiutes who believed in the new religion of the dance. Wovoka, who was only fourteen years old at the time of his father's death, was taken into the family of a white farmer, David Wilson, and was given the name of Jack Wilson.

But as the years passed, Jack Wilson, or Wovoka, continued to receive revelations as his father had done before him. Once during an eclipse of the sun, he fell asleep and was taken up to the world of the Great Spirit. "When the sun died," he said, "I went up to heaven and saw the Great Spirit and all the people who had died a long time ago. The Great Spirit told me to come back and tell my people they must be good and love one another, and not fight, or steal, or lie. He gave to me a dance to give to my people."

This dance was the Ghost Dance, and it would sweep across the mountains and the prairies of the West like a great flow of waters.

The first Ghost Dance was performed on a dancing ground selected by Wovoka on the Walker Lake reservation, January, 1889. The ceremony was simple, the Indians forming into a large circle, dancing and chanting as they constricted the circle, the circle widening and constricting again and again. The dancing continued for a day and a night, Wovoka sitting in the middle of the circle before a large fire with his head bowed. He wore a white striped coat, a pair of trousers, and moccasins. On the second day he stopped the dancing and described the visions that the Great Spirit had sent to him. Then the dancing commenced again and lasted for three more days.

When a second dance was held soon afterwards, several Utes visited the ceremony out of curiosity. Returning to the reservation, the Utes told the neighboring Bannocks about the ceremony. The Bannocks sent emissaries to the next dance, and so did the Mission and Shastan tribes of California, who had somehow heard of the new Messiah.

Within a few weeks, many Rocky Mountain tribes were dancing the Ghost Dance. The Shoshones at Fort Hall reservation saw a ritual staged by the Bannocks, and were so impressed they sent a delegation of five tribesmen to Nevada to learn the new religion from Wovoka's own lips.

When it spread to Washakie's Wind River reservation, the old Shoshone patriarch ordered the dancing stopped. Yet it was from the Wind River Shoshones that the plains tribes learned of the Ghost Dance religion. Perhaps more than any of the other tribes, the Cheyenne and Sioux felt the need of a Messiah who could lead them back to the days of glory. The story of Wovoka was carried swiftly across the plains.

In the autumn of 1889, a Cheyenne delegate named Porcupine made a journey from Montana to learn more about the Ghost Dance. Almost at the same time, Short Bull, Kicking Bear, and several other medicine men of the Sioux traveled all the way from the Dakotas.

The Sioux accepted the Ghost Dance religion with more fervor than any of the Indians. On their return to the Dakota reservations, each delegate tried to outdo the others describing the wonders of the Messiah. He came down from heaven in a cloud, they said. He showed them a vision of all nations of Indians coming home. The earth would be covered with dust and then a new earth would come upon the old. They must use the sacred red and white paint and the sacred grass to make the vanished buffalo return in great herds.

In the spring of 1890, the Sioux began dancing the Ghost Dance at Pine Ridge, adding new symbols to Wovoka's original ceremony. By June they were wearing ghost shirts made of cotton cloth painted blue around the necks, with bright-colored thunder birds, bows and arrows, suns, moons, and stars emblazoned upon them.

226

Wovoka and T. J. McCoy. For most Indians it was a time without spirit, a time of despair. But on Walker Lake reservation in Nevada, a Paiute named Wovoka dreamed a dream in which he was told by the Great Spirit that the Indians must dance the Ghost Dance if they wished to bring back the old days of glory, the old days of the buffalo. The first Ghost Dance was performed at Walker Lake in January, 1889.

To accompany the dancing they made ghost songs:

The whole world is coming,
A nation is coming, a nation is coming,
The Eagle has brought the message to the tribe.
The father says so, the father says so.
Over the whole earth they are coming,
The buffalo are coming, the buffalo are coming.

It was at this moment of keen excitement that the greatest maker of medicine among the Sioux, Sitting Bull, chose to come forth from his "retirement" near the Standing Rock agency, and join the new religion of the dance.

News of the old war-maker's action soon reached General Nelson Miles, commanding the Department of the Missouri. At a chance meeting with Buffalo Bill Cody, the General told the scout about a report he had received from the Pine Ridge agency. "The Ghost Dance craze," said Miles, "has reached such proportions that it's now entirely beyond the control of the Indian agent and the police force."

Cody asked the General if he knew who was behind the movement. Miles guessed that it might be Sitting Bull.

"How about giving me an order for his arrest?" suggested Buffalo Bill.

"Why not? You've known the old rascal for years. He might listen to you, when under the same conditions he'd take a shot at one of my soldiers. But if you think you'll need any help, the army will back you up."

"All I'll need is a wagon load of candy," said Buffalo Bill. "Sitting Bull always did have a weakness for sweets."

Bill Cody proceeded at once to Fort Yates on the Standing Rock reservation, but the military authorities there were opposed to the scout's plans to arrest the Sioux leader. They thought the act might cause more trouble than it would prevent. The officers in com-

Kicking Bear. When the Sioux heard about the Ghost Dance, they sent Kicking Bear and other medicine men on a long journey from the Dakotas to Nevada to learn the dance from the new Messiah.

mand decided to get Buffalo Bill drunk, send a wire to Washington, and have his orders rescinded.

As Captain A. R. Chapin has said: "All officers were requested to assist in drinking Buffalo Bill under the table. But his capacity was such that it took practically all of us in details of two or three at a time to keep him interested and busy throughout the day."

And even though the rugged Cody managed to keep a clear head through all this maneuvering, he had scarcely started out to Sitting Bull's encampment before the order came postponing the arrest. Buffalo Bill returned to Fort Yates, and so ended his part of the affair.

Meanwhile the reservation agent, James McLaughlin, had decided to take Sitting Bull into custody himself, and thus prevent a dangerous disturbance which he feared would result if the military authorities forced the issue and tried to make an arrest. McLaughlin gave the necessary orders to his Indian police, instructing them not to permit the chief to escape under any circumstances.

Just before daybreak on the morning of December 15, 1890, forty-three Indian police surrounded Sitting Bull's log cabin. Lieutenant Bull Head, the Indian policeman in charge of the party, found Sitting Bull asleep on the floor. When he was awakened, the old chieftain stared incredulously at Bull Head. "What you want here?" he asked.

"You my prisoner," said Bull Head calmly. "You must go to agency."

Sitting Bull yawned and sat up. "All right," he said, "I'll dress and go with you." He called one of his wives and sent her to an adjoining cabin for his best clothes, and then asked one of the policemen to saddle his horse for him. While these things were being done, the police began searching for weapons. Two rifles and several knives were seized, and this action evidently angered Sitting Bull, because he began abusing all the police within hearing distance.

About the same time, his ardent followers who had

Sitting Bull. In this time of excitement over the Ghost Dance, Sitting Bull, the greatest maker of medicine among the Sioux, came out of his enforced retirement and joined the new religion. He is shown in this photo at Fort Randall with his two wives, Seen-By-Her-Nation and Four Times, and three children.

been dancing the Ghost Dance every night for weeks were gathering around the cabin. They outnumbered the police four to one, and soon had them pressed against the walls. As soon as Sitting Bull was brought outside, he must have sensed the explosive quality of the situation. Suddenly he turned on Lieutenant Bull Head and told him he was not going to Fort Yates. Then a dramatic gesture of his hands, he called on his followers to rescue him.

Responding immediately, an Indian named Catch-the-Bear fired point-blank at Lieutenant Bull Head, wounding him in the side. As Bull Head fell, he tried to shoot his assailant, but the bullet struck Sitting Bull instead. Almost simultaneously one of the sergeants, Red Tomahawk, shot Sitting Bull through the head. A wild fight developed almost immediately, with the trained police having difficulty holding their own. Only the timely arrival of a cavalry detachment saved them from total extinction.

Big Foot's Band. Many of Sitting Bull's followers fled after his death to join forces with Big Foot's band on the Cheyenne River. They were frightened, but they believed the prophecy of the Messiah was coming true. Soon the earth would be covered with dust, and a new earth would be born. All the nations of Indians long dead would come back to life. The white man would disappear and the buffalo would return. (Nearly all the Indians in this photo were killed at Wounded Knee.)

II

The great Sitting Bull was dead! The news spread like a grass fire across the prairies. Most of the frightened followers of the Hunkpapa leader immediately came into Standing Rock agency and surrendered. Others fled west.

Those who were fleeing west knew exactly where they were going. They were seeking to join forces with a Ghost Dance believer, an old chieftain named Big Foot. Big Foot for some time had been gathering followers at a small village near the mouth of Deep Creek, a few miles below the fork of the Cheyenne River. As the Ghost Dance craze had increased, so had Big Foot's forces, and even before the fatal shooting of Sitting Bull, a small party of cavalrymen had been assigned to watch his movements.

As soon as the news of Sitting Bull's death reached Big Foot, he began preparations to break camp. The cavalry commander, Colonel E. V. Sumner, accepted Big Foot's explanation that the Indians were preparing to proceed to Standing Rock to go on the reservation for the winter. However, a patrol watch was kept on Big Foot's journey. When the band of Sioux fleeing from Sitting Bull's camp joined the new leader, Colonel Sumner again decided to question Big Foot as to his intentions.

The chief was unusually friendly, and declared that the only reason he had been permitted the band from Sitting Bull's camp to join his people was that he felt sorry for them, and wanted them to return to the reservation with him. For a second time, Summer accepted the explanation. In fact the Indians all seemed so friendly that they were permitted to keep their arms—a decision which was to precipitate the tragedy of Wounded Knee.

Before dawn the next day, December 23, Big Foot and his ever-increasing band were in rapid flight, moving in the opposite direction from the Standing Rock reservation. They were heading for the Bad Lands.

Perhaps Big Foot did not know that Kicking Bear and Short Bull had withdrawn to the Bad Lands. But it is a fact that a few days earlier those two leaders, who had once visited the Ghost Dance Messiah in Nevada, were in the Bad Lands. And they had with them about three thousand fanatical followers, keyed up to a high frenzy as a result of their continual dances.

No matter what Big Foot did or did not know, trouble was certainly brewing now.

Moving swiftly to prevent an escape to the Bad Lands, the military authorities ordered S. M. Whitside of the Seventh Cavalry to intercept the Indians. As soon as these cavalrymen were sighted by Big Foot, he sent out mounted Indians with a white flag to meet them. When Major Whitside insisted on parleying with Big Foot, the chief rode out in a wagon.

As he approached Major Whitside, Big Foot

Short Bull. Short Bull, one of the leaders in the Ghost Dance religion, led a group of warriors to the Bad Lands. Kicking Bear also led a band to the Bad Lands, and there were rumors of a new Indian war.

234

seemed to regard the entire affair as a fine joke. "We parley," he said.

The Major shook his head. "No parley," he replied sternly. "Unconditional surrender."

Big Foot considered this abrupt demand for a moment, then nodded acceptance. When Major Whitside gave him orders to lead his people back to Wounded Knee Creek and make camp, Big Foot complied to the letter.

During the ensuing march, none of the cavalrymen suspected that anything was amiss, not one could have guessed what the fates were preparing for the following day on the banks of Wounded Knee Creek. The Indians seemed to be in good humor, they talked and laughed with the soldiers, and smoked their cigarettes. But not one of the cavalrymen seemed to have been aware that all of these Indians were wearing sacred ghost shirts which they believed would protect them from the white man's weapons. And the soldiers seemed to be completely ignorant of the fact that their prisoners were fanatically certain the day of the Indians' return to power was close at hand.

Big Foot had fallen ill from exposure, and rode in his wagon litter. No one paid any particular attention to the chief medicine man, Yellow Bird, who all during the march was moving stealthily up and down the line, occasionally blowing on an eaglebone whistle, and muttering Ghost Dance chants.

When they reached Wounded Knee, the Indians were assigned an area near the cavalry camp. They were carefully counted. One hundred twenty men and two hundred thirty women and children were present. Rations were issued, and they set up their shelters for the night. For additional cover, Major Whitside gave them several army tents. The troop surgeon, John van R. Hoff, was sent to attend the ailing Big Foot, and a stove was set up in the chief's tent.

Whitside revealed, however, that he did not entirely trust Big Foot's band. He posted a battery of four

Hotchkiss guns, training them directly on the Indians' camp.

It was a cold night. Ice was already an inch thick on the tree-bordered creek, and there was a hint of snow in the air.

During the night, Colonel James W. Forsyth of the Seventh Cavalry rode in with additional troops and took command. With Forsyth came a young lieutenant, James D. Mann, who was to witness the opening shots of the approaching battle.

"The next morning," Mann said afterwards, "we started to disarm them, the bucks being formed in a semi-circle in front of the tents. We went through the tents searching for arms, and while this was going on,

Ghost Shirt. The Indians at Wounded Knee wore ghost shirts, magic shirts with bright-colored thunderbirds and buffaloes emblazoned upon them. They believed that the ghost shirts would protect them from the white man's weapons, even from the powerful Hotchkiss guns that were trained on their camp.

236

everyone seemed to be good-natured, and we had no thought of trouble. The squaws were sitting on bundles concealing guns and other arms. We lifted them as tenderly and treated them as nicely as possible.

"As soon as we had finished this search, the squaws began packing up, which was a suspicious sign.

"While this was going on, the medicine man, who was in the center of the semi-circle of bucks, had been going through the Ghost Dance, and making a speech, the substance of which was, as told me by an interpreter afterwards, 'I have made medicine of the white man's ammunition. It is good medicine, and his bullets can not harm you, as they will not go through your ghost shirts, while your bullets will kill.'

"It was then that I had a peculiar feeling come over me which I can not describe—some presentiment of trouble—and I told the men to 'be ready: there is going to be trouble.' We were only six or eight feet from the Indians and I ordered my men to fall back.

"In front of me were four bucks—three armed with rifles and one with bow and arrows. I drew my revolver and stepped through the line to my place with my detachment. The Indians raised their weapons over their heads to heaven as if in votive offering, then brought them down to bear on us, the one with the bow and arrow aiming directly at me. Then they seemed to wait an instant.

"The medicine man threw a handful of dust in the air, put on his war bonnet, and an instant later a gun was fired. This seemed to be the signal they had been waiting for, and the firing immediately began. I ordered my men to fire, and the reports were almost simultaneous."

The surviving Indians told a different version of the outbreak of firing, but both sides agreed that things happened fast after that first volley of shots. The Hotchkiss guns opened fire and began pouring their two-pound explosive shells into the crowd at the rate of nearly fifty per minute, mowing down everything alive. In a few moments, two hundred Indian men,

After the Battle. It is not known who fired the first shot in the Battle of Wounded Knee. The soldiers said that a medicine man there threw a handful of dust into the air as a signal for the Indians to attack. The Indian survivors said that the soldiers fired the first shot. Whatever the cause, it was a bloody battle. Two hundred Indians—men, women, and children—and sixty soldiers were casualties within a few minutes.

women and children and sixty soldiers were lying dead and wounded on the ground, the ripped tipis blazing and smoking around them. Some of the surviving Indians fled to the nearby ravine, hiding among the rocks and scrub cedars. Others continued their flight up the slopes to the south.

On the bloody campground, Surgeon John van R. Hoff did what he could for the wounded. He disarmed a wounded Indian who was still trying to fire his rifle. The warrior staggered to his feet, looked down fixedly at the body of Yellow Bird, the medicine man who was responsible for inciting the attack. "If I could be taken to you," the wounded Indian muttered to the dead medicine man, "I would kill you again."

Disillusionment over the failure of the ghost shirts had already affected most of the others. One of the squaws tore off her brilliantly colored shirt and stamped upon it while blood flowed from her wounds and trickled down into the dust.

Dead Chief. Big Foot, the Sioux leader, was found dead, frozen grotesquely where he had fallen.

As it was obvious by the end of the day that a blizzard was approaching, the medical staff began gathering the wounded together, and they were carried in to a field hospital at Pine Ridge. Twenty-five soldiers and one hundred fifty-three or more Indians had died. The exact total of the latter would never be known because a great snowstorm was blanketing the South Dakota plains.

When the burial party went out to Wounded Knee after the blizzard, they found many of the bodies frozen grotesquely where they had fallen. All the Indians were buried together in a large pit, and a few days later their tribesmen came and put up a wire fence around the trench and smeared the posts with sacred red medicine paint.

But the vision of the peaceful Paiute dreamer, Wovoka, had come to an end with the Battle of Wounded Knee. And so had all the long and tragic years of Indian resistance on the western plans.

The Dead. End of the Ghost Dance. The Indians who died at Wounded Knee were buried together in a large pit. Later their tribesmen built a wire fence around the grave, smearing the posts with sacred red medicine paint.

240

Pine Ridge Agency, 1891. The vision of
Wovoka, the Ghost Dance Messiah, had
ended, and with it ended Indian resistance on
the western plains. The Indians knew that
wars and battles and raids must be forever
ended. Their future lay on the great
reservations.

The Living. The chiefs who survived agreed
that the trail of the Indian had run into the
road of the white man. Perhaps the white
man would show them that his road was
better. They would wait and see.

BIBLIOGRAPHY

Arnold, Frazer, "Ghost Dance and Wounded Knee," *Cavalry Journal,* 43 (May/June, 1934), 19–20.

Arnold, R. Ross, *Indian Wars of Idaho,* Caldwell, Idaho, 1932.

Bancroft, Hubert H., *History of Arizona and New Mexico,* San Francisco, 1889.

Bourke, John G., *An Apache Campaign in the Sierra Madre,* New York, 1886.

Bourke, John G., *Mackenzie's Last Fight with the Cheyennes,* Governor's Island, N.Y., 1890.

Bourke, John G., *On the Border with Crook,* New York, 1891.

Brill, Charles J., *Conquest of the Southern Plains,* Oklahoma City, 1938.

Brininstool, Earl A., *Fighting Red Cloud's Warriors,* Columbus, Ohio, 1926.

Carrington, Frances C., *My Army Life and the Fort Phil Kearney Massacre,* Philadelphia, 1910.

Carrington, Henry B., *Ab-Sa-Ra-Ka* (Third Edition of Mrs. Margaret Irvin Carrington's Narrative), Philadelphia, 1878.

Carter, Robert G., *On the Border with Mackenzie,* Washington, D.C., 1935.

Clum, Woodworth, *Apache Agent,* Boston, 1936.

Crook, George, *Autobiography* (Manuscript), Army War College Library, Washington, D.C.

Crook, George, *Resume of Operations against Apache Indians, 1882 to 1886,* Omaha, 1886.

Cruse, Thomas, *Apache Days and After,* Caldwell, Idaho, 1941.

Custer, George A., *Wild Life on the Plains and Horrors of Indian Warfare,* St. Louis, 1891.

Davis, Britton, *The Truth about Geronimo,* New Haven, 1929.

Dunn, Jacob P., *Massacres of the Mountains, a History of the Indian Wars of the Far West,* New York, 1886.

Dustin, Fred, *The Custer Tragedy,* Ann Arbor, Mich., 1939.

Ellis, A. N., "Recollections of an Interview with Cochise, Chief of the Apaches." *Kansas State Historical Society Collections, XIII* (Topeka, Kan., 1915), 387–392.

Fee, Chester A., *Chief Joseph, the Biography of a Great Indian,* New York, 1936.

Finerty, John F., *War-path and Bivouac,* Chicago, 1890.

Graham, William A., *The Story of the Little Big Horn,* Harrisburg, Pa., 1941.

Grinnell, George B., *The Fighting Cheyennes,* New York, 1915.

Grinnell, George B., *Two Great Scouts and their Pawnee Battalion,* Cleveland, 1928.

Hebard, Grace R., and Brininstool, Earl A., *The Bozeman Trail,* Cleveland, 1922.

Hebard, Grace R., *Washakie,* Cleveland, 1930.

Hodge, Frederick W., *Handbook of American Indians North of Mexico,* Washington, D.C., 1907–1910.

Howard, Helen A., *War Chief Joseph,* Caldwell, Idaho, 1941.

Howard, Oliver O., *Famous Indian Chiefs I Have Known,* New York, 1908.

Howard, Oliver O., *My Life and Experiences among Our Hostile Indians,* Hartford, Conn., 1907.

Hyde, George E., *Red Cloud's Folk,* Norman, Okla., 1937.

Lockwood, Frank C., *The Apache Indians,* New York, 1938.

Luce, Edward S., *Keogh, Comanche and Custer,* St. Louis, 1939.

Miles, Nelson A., *Personal Recollections and Observations,* Chicago, 1896.

Mills, Anson, *My Story,* Washington, D.C., 1918.

Mooney, James, *The Ghost-Dance Religion,* Washington, 1896.

Nickerson, Azor H., *Major General George Crook and the Indians* (Manuscript), Army War College Library, Washington, D.C., n.d.

Ogle, Ralph H., *Federal Control of the Western Apaches, 1848–1886,* Albuquerque, N.M., 1940.

Payne, Doris Palmer, *Captain Jack, Modoc Renegade,* Portland, Ore., 1938.

Rankin, M. Wilson, *Reminiscences of Frontier Days,* Denver, 1935.

Report of a Board of Officers Convened by the Commanding General, Department of the Platte to Examine into and Report the Facts Attending the Arrest, Confinement, Disarmament, Escape and Recapture of a Number of Cheyenne Indians Recently at and in the Vicinity of Fort Robinson, Nebraska. February 7, 1879 (Manuscript), Army War College Library, Washington, D.C.

Richardson, Rupert N., *The Comanche Barrier to South Plains Settlement,* Glendale, Calif., 1933.

Riddle, Jeff C. D., *The Indian History of the Modoc War and the Causes that Led to It,* San Francisco, 1914.

Rister, Carl C., *Border Command; General Phil Sheridan in the West,* Norman, Okla., 1944.

Robinson, Doane, *A History of the Dakota or Sioux Indians,* Aberdeen, S.D., 1904.

Sandoz, Mari, *Crazy Horse,* New York, 1942.

Sass, Herbert R., *Hear Me, My Chiefs,* New York, 1940.

Taft, Robert, *Photography and the American Scene,* New York, 1942.

Tilghman, Zoe A., *Quanah, the Eagle of the Comanches,* Oklahoma City, 1938.

U. S. Bureau of American Ethnology, *Seventeenth Annual Report, Part I,* Washington, D.C., 1898.

U. S. Congress. 43rd. 1st Sess. House Document 122. (Copies of the Correspondence and Paper Relative to the War with the Modoc Indians in Southern Oregon and Northern California, during the Years 1872 and 1873), Washington, D.C., 1874.

U. S. Congress. 44th. 2nd Sess. Senate Ex. Document 9. (Message from the President of the United States Communicating the Report and Journal of the Proceedings of the Commission Appointed to Obtain Certain Concessions from the Sioux Indians), Washington, D.C., 1877.

U. S. Congress. 46th. 2nd Sess. Senate Report 708. (Report of the Select Committee to Examine into the Circumstances Connected With the Removal of the Northern Cheyennes from the Sioux Reservations to the Indian Territory), Washington, D.C., 1880.

U. S. Congress. 50th. 1st Sess. Senate Ex. Document 33. (Indian Operations on the Plains), Washington, D.C., 1887.

U. S. War Dept., *Report of the Secretary of War, 1880, Part I,* Washington, D.C., 1880.

Van de Water, Frederic F., *Glory-Hunter, a Life of General Custer,* Indianapolis, 1934.

Vestal, Stanley, *Sitting Bull,* Boston, 1932.

Vestal, Stanley, *Warpath,* Boston, 1934.

Wharton, Clarence, *Satanta; the Great Chief of the Kiowas and His People,* Dallas, Texas, 1935.

PHOTO CREDITS